A Director's Guide

GW01080785

Family businesses

HOW DIRECTORS CAN MANAGE KEY ISSUES IN A FAMILY FIRM

Editor, Director Publications: Tom Nash
Managing Editor: Lesley Shutte
Production Manager: Victoria Davies
Head of Business Development: Simon Seward
Design: Halo Design
Chairman: Tim Melville-Ross
Managing Director: Andrew Main Wilson

Published for the Institute of Directors and Grant Thornton
by Director Publications Ltd
116 Pall Mall London SW1Y 5ED

Editorial: 0171 766 8910
Sponsorship: 0171 766 8885
Production: 0171 766 8960
Facsimile: 0171 766 8990

YOURS TO HAVE AND TO HOLD
BUT NOT TO COPY

Director Publications Ltd
116 Pall Mall
London SW1Y 5ED

Kogan Page Ltd
120 Pentonville Road
London N1 9JN

© Director Publications 1998

British Library Cataloguing in Publication Data
A CIP record for this book is available from the British Library
ISBN 0 7494 2947 X

Printed and bound in Great Britain by St Ives plc

INSTITUTE OF DIRECTORS

The successful family business: how to manage the key issues

TUESDAY 24 NOVEMBER 1998

▶ Ian Hamilton Fazey

▶ Andrew Godfrey
GRANT THORNTON

▶ Dr Caryn Solomon
BUSINESS PSYCHOLOGIST

▶ Stephen Purdew
HENLOW GRANGE

▶ Steven McBride
THE FAMILY BUSINESS
CONSULTANCY LTD.

▶ Graeme Whittaker
EDDIE STOBART GROUP LTD.

▶ Richard Burns
HAMMOND SUDDARDS

▶ John Newman
SMITH & WILLIAMSON

▶ Conflict

▶ Tax efficiency

▶ Shareholder value

▶ Wealth preservation

▶ Succession

▶ Exit routes

Grant Thornton 🖘

A ONE-DAY CONFERENCE

DIRECTOR CONFERENCES

THE SUBJECT:

The successful family business: how to manage the key issues

THE DATE:

Tuesday 24 November 1998

THE VENUE:

Institute of Directors, 116 Pall Mall, London SW1

THE BACKGROUND:

76% per cent of UK companies are family owned. It is also a fact that only 30% of family businesses reach the second generation and only one in ten make it to the third.

This conference will address the practical issues involved in running a family business and the psychological obstacles which could hinder the growth of your company. It will examine the difficult dynamics, relationships and hidden agendas which drive a family business.

You will learn how to:

▶ *manage the overlap between commercial and family values*
▶ *identify the drivers of relationships within a family business*
▶ *resolve conflict as it arises*
▶ *decide when you should appoint an outsider*
▶ *balance ownership returns versus business investment*
▶ *extract profit tax efficiently*
▶ *preserve wealth and maximise on shareholder value*
▶ *execute a strategic succession plan*
▶ *examine the option of a trade sale*

Breakfast is served from 08.00 in the Brasserie at 116 Pall Mall and is included within the registration fee.

In addition case study speakers will give delegates the benefit of their experience and the Eddie Stobart story will reveal how this family business has grown at a compound rate of 20% since 1988.

Who should attend

All directors and shareholders of family-owned businesses. In view of the subject matter, it would be most beneficial for different generations, spouses and siblings from the same family to attend together. Discounts for multiple bookings are available.

The conference is open to both members and non-members. If you are a member of the IoD you may bring a non-member to this conference at the member rate.

Delegates will receive complementary copies of the director's guide to family businesses which is **produced in association with Grant Thornton**.

THE SPEAKERS

IAN HAMILTON FAZEY has been a Financial Times journalist since 1980. He chairs the annual series of Export Forums staged by Natwest and the FT. He completed 10 years as the FT's northern correspondent in 1996 and now travels extensively, writing for the paper, the OECD and several UN agencies.

ANDREW GODFREY acts as financial adviser to a number of companies and is also a corporate finance partner. Nationally, Andrew is head of growth and development for Grant Thornton. Andrew was responsible for the development of PRIMA, Grant Thornton's consulting service aimed at addressing people and relationship issues in the management of the family owned businesses.

DR CARYN SOLOMON is a qualified psychologist who has vast experience of dealing with conflict and difficult relationship issues in family businesses worldwide. Other areas of specialisation include the transformation of organisational culture, design and implementation of strategic change processes, leadership and management development and coaching.

STEPHEN PURDEW aged 39, is the joint owner along with his mother Dorothy, aged 67 of the famous health farm group that includes Henlow Grange, Forest Mere and Springs Health Farm. This is a family owned and run business employing nearly 1000 staff and with a turnover approaching £20m per annum.

STEVEN MCBRIDE has worked for some 20 years in management consultancy in the USA and the UK. He is a founder of The Family Business Consultancy Ltd, which specialises in assisting family owned businesses to develop their businesses through improved interpersonal relations and management practices.

GRAEME WHITTAKER is a chartered accountant and member of the Institute of Taxation. Ex KPMG and Arthur Anderson, he also spent 14 years with Grant Thornton. He joined Eddie Stobart in 1998 as a group director after acting for them for 4 years as a tax and corporate finance advisor. The Group currently turns over in excess of £100m and employs just short of 2000 people.

RICHARD BURNS is head of corporate finance at Hammond Suddards and specialises in a wide range of mergers and aquisitions work, including the acquisition and disposal of private companies. He also advises extensively on the contractual relationship between shareholders and disputes that arise between shareholders.

JOHN NEWMAN is ex Coopers & Lybrand and Touche Ross & Co. He set up and managed his own practice from 1976 to 1986 when it merged into a London based medium sized firm. He joined Smith & Williamson in 1994 as a corporate tax partner and has experience ranging across many areas of taxation consultancy including family firms in lighting, banking, publishing and other diverse areas.

BOOKING FORM

Family Business (24/11/98)

Surname: (MR/MRS/MS)

First Names:

Membership No: (IF APPLICABLE)

Job Title:

Company:

Address:

Postcode:

Telephone:

Fax:

Please reserve a place for me at the conference
(All fees include VAT @ 17.5%)

Bookings received by 26/10/98:

Members:	£311.00 per delegate
Non-Members:	£375.00 per delegate

Bookings received after 26/10/98:

Members:	£345.00 per delegate
Non-Members:	£416.00 per delegate

I am paying by □ Cheque □ Switch □ Credit Card

□ Visa □ Access
□ Diners Club □ Amex
□ IoD Visa Gold Card

Card No:

Name on Card:

Expiry Date:

Signature:

Date:

For office use only: A B

NETWORKING

Networking is one of the main benefits of attending conferences. To increase the networking opportunities available to delegates attending IoD conferences, the Institute produces a networking brochure in association with most programmes. The brochure gives each delegate the opportunity to advertise his or her company, free of charge, to other delegates. To ensure that your business is included in the brochure circulated to delegates on 24 November, please complete the form below and return to Director Conferences by 9 November.

Delegate:

Company:

Job Title:

Description of Company
(APPROXIMATELY 45 WORDS)

Contact:

Telephone:

DELEGATE BENEFITS

£25 DISCOUNT	on attendance fee at any future IoD conference
UP TO 25% DISCOUNT	on books & magazines purchased from Director Publications
FREE ADVERTISEMENT	in *Networking at IoD Conferences* (see details overleaf)
FREE REFRESHMENTS	during the day, to include English breakfast, three course lunch with coffee/tea
DELEGATE PORTFOLIO	containing conference documentation and speakers' papers as supplied

REGISTRATION DETAILS AND PROCEDURE

Please complete the booking form overleaf and send with payment (payable to Director Conferences) to:

Director Conferences, 116 Pall Mall, London SW1Y 5ED
Tel: 0171 766 8920. Fax: 0171 766 8987
E-mail: conferences@iod.co.uk Web site: http://www.iod.co.uk

Note: All fees must be paid in advance of the conference. Telephone bookings cannot be accepted.

If you wish to book a conference place for more than one delegate please photocopy the booking form.

MULTIPLE BOOKING

These qualify for discounts if three or more delegates from the same company wish to attend. Details available on request.

CANCELLATIONS

These will only be accepted if received *in writing* more than 30 days before the date of the conference. All fees are forfeited thereafter. Substitutions may be made but, if the substitute is a non-member, any fee difference must be paid.

REFRESHMENTS

Breakfast, lunch and appropriate coffee/tea breaks are included in the delegate fee. Please advise of special dietary requirements. (Orders for full English breakfast should be placed before 08.15)

Director Conferences reserves the right to cancel any event, in which case full refunds will be made. Programmes and timings may be subject to change.

09.00	**Registration and coffee**
09.30	**Opening remarks by the chairman** Ian Hamilton Fazey
09.40	**The dynamics of a family business** Andrew Godfrey, Grant Thornton
10.20	**The psychology of the family business** **Getting the family to work together and dealing with conflict** Dr Caryn Solomon, Business Psychologist
11.00	**Coffee/tea**
11.30	**Case study:** *Two generations working together* Stephen Purdew, Henlow Grange
12.00	**Succession management and exit routes** **Grooming the business for sale** Steven McBride, The Family Business Consultancy Ltd
12.45	**Lunch**
14.00	**Case study:** *The Eddie Stobart story* Graeme Whittaker, Eddie Stobart Group Ltd
14.40	**Addressing the legal concerns** **Shareholders agreements** Richard Burns, Hammond Suddards
15.20	**Special taxation issues affecting family businesses** **Preserving wealth** John Newman, Smith & Williamson
16.00	**Conclusion and close of conference**

Keeping it in the family

Tim Melville-Ross, Director General, Institute of Directors

Family businesses are big business, now representing a far greater proportion of the economy than ever before. However, little is actually known about them and the prospects and problems that they face.

This Director's Guide identifies the critical issues that any family business will need to address as it grows and prospers, from implementing secure financial structures to preserving wealth.

Perhaps more importantly, it investigates the unique culture of the family firm, acknowledging the frictions that are caused by working with family members, and outlining effective ways to resolve conflict.

To succeed, the family business must attend to the distinct needs and roles of family members involved in the business, those members of the family that are outside of the business, and employees of the business who do not belong to the family.

The guide also aims to defuse flash-points that occur even for the more established family firm, such as the transfer of a family business from one generation to the next – an area which, when mishandled, is a frequent cause of family business failure.

Succession planning is now the single biggest issue for the family business. While it is not always easy, companies need to devote a significant amount of time to ensuring that their chief executive has a choice of potentially suitable successors. Above all, succession plans need to be openly discussed and understood by everyone within the business.

The linchpin of the economy

Claire Oldfield, small business correspondent, The Sunday Times

Family businesses are the unsung heroes of the economy: they are dynamic, entrepreneurial, provide jobs and most of them expect to grow. Indeed, there are already a handful that have made the transition from micro-businesses through medium-sized enterprises, to become stockmarket giants like Sainsbury.

But the problems family firms face in attempting to combine business nous with family politics are unique, often explosive, and can prevent them achieving their full potential. The statistics suggest that, in the main, family businesses are fragile entities with only 24 per cent surviving to the second generation and just 14 per cent making it to the third.

One of the main barriers to their longevity and growth is a lack of advice when they encounter teething troubles, sibling rivalries or a succession problem.

This guide aims to plug this advice gap by acknowledging that family firms are distinct from other small firms and partnerships. It also provides an excellent outline of the culture of family firms and the environment in which they operate.

It is clear that family enterprises play a fundamental part in society. But if they are to continue to provide jobs, supply exports and create wealth, they must be supported as a unique sector of the economy. So far relatively little research has been carried out into family-run businesses, which is why this guide – which is specifically aimed at helping to preserve family businesses – is so important to a continued understanding of the sector.

Chapter 1

Family businesses in Britain

Professor Sue Birley of Imperial College Management School, and Professor Bridget Rosewell of Business Strategies Limited, identify the core characteristics that define a family business

Suddenly it has become fashionable to be a family business. They are now extolled as the lifeblood of the economy, just as a decade or so ago, it was big business that was all the rage (and on which all government policy was focused).

So, what is a family business? Put simply, it is a business that has some form of family involvement. But what do we mean by involvement? Let us suggest some possibilities and see if you agree:

- *Two brothers form and run a business. They both own some equity;*

- *One person founds the business, but the spouse also has equity. The children are in their teens;*

- *Two founder families own equity in a publicly quoted company, but continue to manage the company;*

- *The children of the founder inherit equity in the business, but pursue their own careers;*

- *The business is run by a professional manager who may or may not have shares, but the family controls the board;*

- *The first and second-generation members of the family are employed in the business, but only the first has equity.*

Some of you may argue that it depends on the amount of equity that the family owns: to be a family business, the family must own at least 50 per cent. Others may feel that if the founding family controls managerial succession, it doesn't matter how much equity the family members own. Then again, one could say that a family business involves more than a single generation in the management.

It is usual to think of family businesses in the same breath as small and medium-sized enterprises (SMEs), even though some "family businesses" are actually very large; it is only recently that the last Sainsbury has left the board of the family firm. However, to a large extent, this is not unreasonable: most smaller businesses are unlikely to be listed on the Stock Exchange and are more likely to be privately owned and controlled. Many of these will also see themselves as family businesses – even if this term has no precise meaning.

Irrespective of their size, such businesses are becoming increasingly important. After decades of large companies "downsizing", smaller and family owned businesses are a much greater proportion of the economy than ever before. Even the definition of a small business has been reduced; the EU has recently changed its definition from those employing between 10 and 500 people, to those employing below 250.

At the extreme, you could claim that all closely held businesses are family businesses, since the business is the source of income, wealth, and pension for all members of the family, future or present, working in the business or not. The point is that there are no rules that categorically define this group. However, each of the above definitions reflects a series of personal decisions as to the way that the relationship between the business and the family is managed.

Quite simply, if you believe that you are running, or working in, a family business – whatever the equity or managerial structure – then it is likely that you are. In your view, decisions are being made which take account of family considerations, and vice versa – and you are probably not alone.

THE IMPORTANCE OF FAMILY BUSINESSES

One of the few sources of information regarding the prospects and problems of family businesses is the Grant Thornton/Business Strategies European Business Survey, which has been conducted since 1993. Half the UK businesses surveyed operate in more than one location, with 23 per cent having operations in other EU countries and ten per cent in North America. The picture of such businesses being single site, perhaps rather sleepy operations, seems to be wide of the mark.

Family businesses are not just the bedrock of much of the economy, providing as much as 30 per cent of all employment; they expect to grow. Furthermore, they also have wide-ranging attitudes to the markets in which they operate. Nearly half engage in exporting activity to some extent, and of these, over a third export over a quarter of their turnover. Almost all exporters trade with other EU countries and nearly half trade with North America and with Asia/Pacific countries. This international outlook reflects companies' understanding that competitive pressure is increasing everywhere: nationally, locally and in other EU countries.

MANAGEMENT SKILLS

So far, we have painted a buoyant picture of UK family businesses – they operate in a wide variety of markets and with optimistic and well-supported plans for expansion.

According to the companies, the main fly in the ointment is a lack of management skills. In the survey, this was cited as the most important constraint on their ability to expand – more important even than a shortage of orders, which has been the most important constraint up to now. A similar result applies to the long term, where management succession ranks alongside limited market demand as the main constraint.

It is not clear why this should be the case. It may be that even in family oriented businesses, management is seen as a professional as much as a family activity: in the UK, management teams tend to be bigger, and fewer businesses view themselves as family ones – though family shareholdings remain hugely important. The willingness to view management as a skill which could be in short supply might well be seen as a strength, since this suggests that action will be taken. Indeed, there is evidence that management training is seen as one of the main areas for development.

FAMILY ATTITUDES

A further study of 535 family businesses in the UK, carried out by Imperial College Management School and Grant Thornton, explored respondents' attitudes to a range of family and business issues. They divided almost equally into three groups:

- *The Family Rules Group was very clear that the business was stronger with family involvement, that successors should be chosen from the family and that shares should only be transferred to members of the family;*

- *The Family Out Group believed exactly the opposite; while*

- *The Family Business Jugglers were conscious of trying to balance the interests of both.*

Clearly, what matters in growing and managing a business is not just your attitudes to family involvement, but the way in which these attitudes are translated into action.

For example, a succeeding generation which has been steeped in the business since childhood, that knows the customers, and has been educated to fit the needs of the business, that wants to take the business forward, and is respected by the employees, can provide valuable, long-term stability for the business. Certainly, their timescales for investment are likely to be longer than those of a venture capitalist or the public stockmarket. By contrast, an indulged playboy, with no interest in the business and few managerial skills, is likely to be a disaster as a managing director.

Obviously, both businesses and families are complex organisations with different goals, timescales, emotions and needs. Put them together and the mixture can be explosive. The aims of this book are to try to help the family to address the people and relationship issues of family businesses and to help the directors who are managing the business to avoid some of the elephant traps ahead.

PLANNING FOR THE FUTURE

In conclusion, the evidence suggests that the family business sector in the UK is in a healthy condition – and is taking those aspects of its situation that need improvement seriously. Family businesses operate across the board in sectoral terms and, increasingly, the sector appears to be expanding into new markets and exporting to a wider variety of locations.

However, anyone who owns a business must plan for the future, whatever their attitude to family involvement. If, for example, you belong to the "Family Out" group, you must positively plan to keep them out! You will need to think about long-term ownership, and about transferring equity to others. This means planning a public flotation, a trade sale to another company, or sale to the employees (a management buy-out).

If you are a "Family Rules" advocate, you must plan the family succession – both in terms of training your family to take over managerial responsibility (assuming they want to), and in terms of transferring your equity to the next generation. This means taking both legal advice regarding your estate (making a will) and financial advice regarding, for example, capital gains taxation.

Whatever the road you take, it may well be rocky. Families fight, conduct extended feuds, apply emotional pressure, and have favourites, all of which impact on the business.

Chapter 2

The culture of family firms

What are the unique features of a family business culture, and what are the potential effects on its success? Andrew Godfrey, head of growth and development services at Grant Thornton, provides some insights

Family firms face the same economic issues as all businesses, including market and technological changes, shifting customer tastes, ever tougher competition and political instability. However, their financial capability is often more limited and, in addition, they have less management depth than larger companies to cope with these pressures.

The difficulties inherent in balancing the goals and the needs of the family with those of the business have a further impact on the company and its ability to perform in the marketplace. For instance, the traditional divide between ownership (seeking dividend income) and management (seeking reinvestment for growth and future profitability) may be aggravated by differing family views of the future, in terms of whether to "cash in the chips" or "hang in for the long run".

Traditionally, analysis has focused on the individual as the emotionally meaningful unit, with the family viewed as a collection of related individuals. However, for the purpose of understanding the family business, it is more appropriate to study families as a unit, with their own structures, beliefs and patterns of relating. Indeed, the underlying issues facing the family and its business need to be properly understood, otherwise resolutions to problems may be deemed inappropriate or simply not feasible.

To unlock the deepest and most lasting solutions, one must understand the interactions between family members, family dynamics and address the psychological issues that hold the solutions captive.

OVERLAPPING THE FAMILY AND BUSINESS SYSTEMS

One of the key advantages of a family business is that a cohesive force usually exists providing a strong sense of mission and a shared vision, ideally cemented by loyalty and commitment. The business may be financed by equity provided by founders or their successors, who are willing to balance the current return on their investment with a long-term strategy and continuation of the family heritage, referred to as "patient" capital.

The benefit of relatively low capital costs allows them to adopt longer-term business strategies, or to exploit market niches which are not sufficiently profitable for larger businesses which require higher short-term returns on capital.

A successful family business is also free of pressures for short-term profits and has the foresight and power to take a long-term perspective, saving and reinvesting capital, and viewing the business as a legacy for its heirs. However, whereas system theory teaches that all aspects (or sub-systems) of a system are interdependent, the family and the business – while containing many of the same people – are vastly different worlds. The family and business each have their own priorities, goals and expectations.

The family is typically inward-looking and, as such, decisions are often based on emotions rather than commercial grounds. This contrasts with business decisions which demand rationality and results. However, it is easy to see why the basis for decision-making differs; there is a history to the family which in terms of each individual pre-dates their involvement in the business. Further, a fully functioning family is likely to incorporate the characteristics of lifetime membership and unconditional acceptance of family members. (See the table opposite for a summary of the respective traits of family and business systems.)

FAMILY VALUES IN THE BUSINESS	
FAMILY SYSTEMS	**BUSINESS SYSTEMS**
Traits	**Traits**
■ Inward looking	■ Outward looking
■ Emotion based	■ Task based
■ Unconditional acceptance	■ Unemotional
■ Sharing	■ Reward performance
■ Lifetime membership	■ Perform or leave
■ Averse to change	■ Embrace change
	■ Conditional acceptance
	■ Conscious behaviour
Tasks	**Tasks**
■ To nurture	■ To generate profits
■ To develop	■ To develop skills
■ To grow adults	

To the extent that the family system and the business system overlap, there is potential for conflict. This arises as the family system seeks to preserve harmony and minimise change, while at the same time the business system needs conflict and change if it is to survive and develop in the long term. Accordingly, where the family and business system overlap, the personal and relationship issues in the family and the management need to be addressed and conflict resolution procedures adopted.

The scope for conflict is increased as the business, the family and the individual all have their own needs, goals and stages of development. However, harmony is a rarity as the stages through which a business progresses are not necessarily in synchronisation with the family's or individual's stages of development. For example, a business may need renewal or revitalisation just when its founder wants to harvest the fruits of his years of work. On the other hand, a business may need renewal and change at a time when the new generation moving into power lacks the skills to accomplish this.

For every business stage the prerequisite managerial skills and abilities are different, and many of the dilemmas faced in family businesses are related to the stage of development of one or more family members. Each of these issues has its own challenges and tasks, and the business can suffer if the family does not face such realities. For instance, many families find it hard to tell the founder that his or her skills are not relevant to the new challenge, or that he has taken his foot off the pedal and is allowing the business to stagnate.

A crucial period for a family business is during expansion. There will come a stage when the family or existing management do not have either the skills or sufficient time to manage the business effectively. At this point, it may be appropriate to introduce external management, which in itself needs careful management and may result in additional friction. The business may operate smoothly under ordinary conditions, but as soon as pressure develops, the family may revert to its natural pattern. This is likely to handicap effective decision-making, which will become bottle-necked. Opportunities will be lost and morale may decline as non-family employees feel disempowered.

When conflicts develop within families, or when circumstances force family enterprises to become liquid, capital costs can increase, turning the competitive advantage of patient capital into a fatal liability. This is most likely to arise when a family business is faced with generational, strategic or ownership transactions. For example:

- *There may be limited available capital to facilitate growth;*

- *Excessive shareholder demands;*

- *The death of a key shareholder may result in a personal cash requirement to pay inheritance tax;*

- *Personal financial problems;*

- *Divorce of a shareholder.*

DEVELOPMENT THROUGH THE GENERATIONS

The typical stages of development for a family business, as it passes on from generation to generation, is for the founder to pass the business on to his or her heirs, usually forming a partnership involving children, who in turn pass on their interests to their own children. Hence, by the third generation the business is managed through a cousins' confederation.

In the second generation there may be conflict between brothers or sisters, due to sibling rivalry. This is considered to be normal, caused by children's desire to win the exclusive love of their parents. However, while there is an underlying assumption that as adults, siblings will take their respective paths in life, in a family business the stage of siblings growing apart is inhibited. Rivalry may be perpetuated through day-to-day contact during business hours or, as is often the case, disagreement over their respective remuneration packages.

Furthermore, primogeniture, the phenomenon of favouring the first born, is often evident in a family business, with elder brothers usually earmarked as their father's successor. Alternatively, conflict may arise from a parent's wish to treat children equally, resulting in the "locking in" of sibling rivalry, through equal ownership of the business.

However, it is generally thought that siblings, despite jealousy and rivalry, actually have a better chance of forming a working business relationship than people who have not grown up together. By the time they are in business together, brothers and sisters – even if they do not love and trust each other – do know how the other thinks, what motivates them and how they respond to pressure, and will usually have developed some conflict resolution skills. Cousins, on the other hand, have no such historical bonds. They belong to different families, and may have different value systems.

A PATH TO SURVIVAL

Problems arising from the overlap of the family and the business should be addressed by developing mechanisms which allow the family to learn to make good business decisions, while achieving family harmony. Accordingly, if the business is to survive and to continue on its path of growth, the "loose methods" of the entrepreneurship or initial stage of the business' life cycle must give way to a more disciplined and structured approach.

The business must be professionalised at all levels, and all processes need to be integrated into a coherent and manageable whole which operates on the basis of sound commercial principles. The essential milestones that a company must pass in evolving towards professionalism are:

- *Adequately documented shareholder agreements;*

- *Agreement on goals and objectives for the business;*

- *Growth rates;*

- *Acceptability of risk levels;*

- *Expected returns on investment;*

- *Timely and accurate accounting information to facilitate planning, operational decision-making and performance review;*

- *A sufficiently skilled and integrated management team.*

In view of family firms' insulation from outside feedback and influences, one powerful solution is to establish a well-constructed board which includes non-executive directors, who will bring an additional dimension to the business. The board should include skills such as management experience, broader business insight and strategic perspective, as well as providing objectivity and promoting performance accountability.

Chapter 3

Resolving conflict

Recognising and resolving conflict requires skill and, at times, expert facilitation. Dr Caryn Solomon of the London Consulting Group offers some guidelines

Most of us are uncomfortable with conflict. We see it as a destructive expression of emotions and as a signal of relationship breakdown. Yet conflict is an inevitable part of human relationships. It is impossible for human beings to spend any significant time together without having some differences, and it is seldom that innovations and improvements are achieved without conflict. In fact, conflict is often a catalyst for change, and an essential factor in maintaining healthy relationships based on open, honest communication.

The first step to constructive conflict resolution is to recognise that conflict need not always be destructive: it is possible to have a "good" fight. The next step is to become aware of some of the key triggers and underlying dynamics of conflict.

THE ORGANISATIONAL ICEBERG

In the context of family businesses, it is useful to think about conflicts which arise in terms of the idea of the "organisational iceberg". Every organisation can be likened to an iceberg, with some aspects above the water: visible, concrete, measurable and relatively easily understood. Often referred to as the "hard issues", these aspects include factors such as the company mission and objectives, organisational structure, systems, technology, products, services, policies, programmes, procedures, financial data and office location and layout.

Below the water are the covert, intangible "soft" aspects of organisational life: people's perceptions, assumptions, attitudes, beliefs, feelings, values and relationships. It is here that we find friendships, enmities, conflicts and power struggles.

The challenge for any business seeking success is to recognise that it is not sufficient to have innovative products and services, cost-focused financial systems, state-of-the-art technology and fancy office buildings. If the foundation of the iceberg is fragile or rotten, if people are stressed and relationships fraught, if the company's values are ill-defined or incompatible with its strategic objectives, if the organisational culture does not enable the business to thrive, the entire iceberg will crumble.

When conflict erupts, no matter what the overt problem appears to be, there is always an underlying, bottom-of-iceberg component which is driving the process and which must be brought to the surface for the conflict to be resolved successfully.

THE FAMILY SYSTEM AND THE BUSINESS SYSTEM

Recognising and understanding the covert issues in any organisation requires skill, and usually expert facilitation. In family businesses, managing conflict is made more difficult because of the complex interaction between the family system and the business system.

Conflicts which seem, on the surface, to be about business issues are often manifestations of underlying assumptions and dynamics within the family. In such cases, it is unlikely that simple business solutions will be sufficient to make the real problem disappear. Sooner or later, it will re-emerge, because the deeper issues will not have been addressed.

For example, common areas of conflict in family businesses are employment and exit policies, salary and bonuses, leadership and control issues and the definition of roles. While these issues may present genuine business-related challenges, they are often further complicated by the fact that family members typically come into the family business with assumptions of "entitlement".

Many children enter the business assuming that they are entitled to a car, free air tickets and fast promotion to senior positions. Conflict often erupts when these expectations are frustrated by a wise parent who recognises the potentially destructive effects on the business of treating children preferentially. On the other hand, it is equally common for conflict to arise between family and non-family employees when such assumptions remain unchallenged.

RELATIONSHIPS WHICH CAUSE CONFLICT

Some of the most dramatic and devastating conflicts in family businesses are the result of psychological factors in two particularly complex sets of relationships.

THE FATHER-SON RELATIONSHIP

Although daughters are becoming more prominent in family businesses, the principal parent-child relationship in business still revolves around fathers and sons. While there are many loving and successful father-son relationships in business, conflict between fathers and sons is one of the principal sources of trouble in family businesses.

Typically, the father wants his sons to follow him and to allow him to lead the business for as long as possible. Few fathers step aside voluntarily. The father's message to the sons is that the business has been built for them and will one day be theirs in its entirety and that, therefore, it is not necessary to demand real money or real power now.

Meanwhile, it is expected that no son should leave the business which the father has worked so hard to build. In this way, many sons are trapped in a situation in which they can neither gain autonomy and independence nor fully take what they are being offered. If they leave, they are seen as ungrateful. If they try to take power they will destroy the father. If they disobey him, they are disloyal and unappreciative.

In many cases, inter-generational conflict is resolved by the passage of time. However, early disagreements often turn into severe situations and should be confronted sooner rather than later. Resolutions should be sought with third-party intervention, where the purpose would be to promote open dialogue as a means of clarifying expectations, sharing feelings and defining roles.

SIBLING RIVALRY

Sibling rivalry is normal, but it can sometimes become a destructive force that threatens the survival of the business when, for example, more than one child aspires to succeed the owner as boss. If the business is large enough, rivalry can be curbed by defining clear and separate areas of responsibility. In addition, siblings themselves can prevent the destructive effects of rivalry by recognising its potential for harm. In addition, they can agree to a conflict resolution process which aims to preserve both the personal relationships and the business, and is assisted by a third party, such as the board of directors or a professional consultant.

CONSTRUCTIVE CONFLICT RESOLUTION

Keeping in mind the need to manage the whole organisational iceberg, the most constructive approach to conflict is for the family to focus on the following objectives:

■   *Planning a future together;*

■   *Addressing critical issues relating to the family's involvement with the business;*

■   *Articulating core values for the business;*

■   *Establishing ongoing processes to resolve conflicts, maintain communication and monitor progress.*

COMMUNICATION IS CRITICAL

If communication is to remain open and honest, the owner must take the lead. Unfortunately, however, many owners resist bringing up sensitive issues which may cause unpleasant conflict, preferring to let sleeping dogs lie. As a result, conflicts often fester until the business passes to the next generation, at which point the likelihood of war breaking out is much greater.

Many owners also tend to be frustratingly secretive regarding financial details and business problems, with the result that children are unable to participate meaningfully or provide assistance and support, speculation becomes rampant and frustrations and tensions build. If the owners and their spouses meet with their children and other family members involved in the business to share and exchange their views openly, it becomes possible for the family to develop unified, integrated approaches to the business. Even if there is disagreement on some issues, at least everyone contributes to the process and understands the ground rules.

THE FAMILY COUNCIL

A successful mechanism to aid conflict resolution within families is the family council which provides a forum for family members to express their concerns, thoughts, feelings, needs and aspirations, and to contribute to goal setting, policy-making and the defining of values. It enables mutual understanding and is an arena within which issues of accountability and responsibility are confronted and explored.

In severely troubled families it is often impossible for people to communicate constructively, and sometimes even to sit in the same room together. These families are better off seeking help from a professional facilitator who may wish to spend time talking to individuals before a family meeting.

Even relatively "healthy" families benefit greatly from the use of a facilitator, whose presence comes to represent a safe environment in which individuals feel comfortable being authentic, open and able to take the risk of bringing up conflicting or controversial issues. A skilled facilitator can assist the leader in offering a model of openness to the perspectives of others, as well as willingness to share his or her own views openly. Individuals will begin to participate openly as they realise that they will be supported rather than criticised or censured.

The composition and timing of the family council is a matter of preference. However, the most effective councils include both active and inactive family members and their spouses, and meetings should start as soon as the children are old enough to enter the business. Experience in this area has shown that quarterly meetings are most beneficial.

THE FAMILY RETREAT

The best way to start your family council is with a one- or two-day retreat in a quiet place away from the business. This provides a relaxed environment within which family members can discuss their future in a constructive way and spend informal time together. This exercise is invaluable in terms of building trust and clearing emotional baggage which may have accumulated.

Here too, employing an experienced family business consultant can guide the process and ensure that it remains constructive. They can also help the family to acknowledge and express critical issues and concerns, and to articulate and decide on alternative paths of action. In addition to whatever individuals wish to discuss, key issues which should be addressed include:

■ *The family's aspirations for the business;*

■ *Management standards for the business;*

■ *Issues of ownership and control;*

■ *Management succession;*

■ *Relationships with each other;*

■ *The role of "outsiders";*

■ *Responsibilities to the community;*

■ *The articulation of core values for the family and the business.*

THE FAMILY CREED

The family's decisions in these areas can be captured in the family creed, a document which spells out the family's values and philosophy and which becomes a blueprint for the future. To ensure its ongoing relevance, it should be reviewed annually and always be subject to modification. At quarterly family council meetings, it is useful to refer to this document as a means of tracking progress and of ensuring commitment to the guiding principles which are considered to be important enough to be part of the family creed.

PROFESSIONALISING THE BUSINESS

For a family business to be successful in the years ahead, it will need to become as professional as their non-family counterparts. This implies a focus on:

- *Maintaining appropriate boundaries between family and business systems;*

- *Thinking strategically about the future of the business;*

- *Attracting, motivating and retaining high-quality employees who are invited to participate in decisions and who are recognised for their performance;*

- *Open, regular communication and participation by employees in defining management goals and standards;*

- *Establishing a positive relationship with a working, independent board of directors consisting of competent advisers who are dedicated to the best interests of the family and the business, and who can help guide the company by providing support for the leader;*

- *Early planning for management succession, where possible, or for alternatives such as selling or dividing the company or installing professional management;*

- *Careful planning of estates;*

- *The establishment of processes to resolve disagreements constructively and the use of outside assistance when needed;*

- *The development of an open, flexible, energetic company culture which is sensitive to internal complexities and to customer needs.*

CONCLUSION

Managing conflict is an ongoing process. It requires sustained energy and a commitment to maintaining an open dialogue which challenges assumptions in a context of mutual acceptance and willingness to share. With a modicum of humility, an open mind and a dash of humour, each player in the family business drama will be revitalised and can, in turn, contribute to the ongoing revitalisation of the family business.

CASE STUDY

Beckie Lawless joined family business City Herbs when she was 19. Today, at 30, she is general manager of a 80-plus strong, £5 million-a-year company that operates from New Spitalfields, supplying fresh produce to 300 corporate clients a day. "My advice for any child thinking of taking the easy option of a job within their family business is 'Don't'," she says.

City Herbs was the classic-structured family firm: set up by Maggie Lawless, in 1984, it quickly took on her brother Richard, then daughter Beckie and her partner Gee (who had worked for a rival family business in the market) and, eventually, Maggie's husband.

Of all the conflicts exclusive to family companies, the issue of siblings working alongside – and competing for jobs – with other employees is the spikiest of thorns. "I still find that I'm discriminated against," says Beckie. "When all the people I work with go out for a drink, the person they don't invite is Beckie Lawless. It's perfectly natural, of course. What fun would there be in going out on a staff jolly if you couldn't gossip like mad about your boss? For me, that still hurts a bit. But it's part of being an integral part of a family business. And, if you don't like it, then hard luck, you've got to lump it."

In time, many conflicts are resolved, simply by the company getting to a size where the employment of non-family professionals is essential. But, when Beckie arrived, the company was not yet mature enough to have given well-defined job structures. "The first couple of years were hell," she recalls. "And the next two weren't much better. I was having to learn every job in the company from everyone else working there. But, I soon discovered, we had a few staff who clearly weren't working as they should. I was 'family' and had no doubts where my loyalties lay, but it made life very difficult.

"The only thing I could do was wait for staff to gradually change. Newcomers looked on me in an entirely different way. In their eyes I was there; established. It's a terrible thing to say, but my lucky break came when my mum became ill for a couple of months. I had to take charge.

"With hindsight, I should have spent a few years working away from City Herbs learning a specific job – personnel, or finance, or whatever – which would have given me a particular skill to bring to the family business.

Chapter 4

Shareholder agreements

Richard Burns, head of corporate finance, Hammond Suddards, highlights the key components that any shareholders' agreement should contain

A shareholders' agreement is a legally binding arrangement entered into between each of the shareholders in a company, by which they agree how their relationship as shareholders will be regulated.

Shareholders' agreements are often drawn up when unrelated business people come together to form a company, for example to create a joint venture. Experience suggests that very few family businesses have a shareholders' agreement in place, but there are two reasons why the participants should consider having one prepared.

First, the process of negotiating and agreeing a shareholders' agreement can be a useful way of bringing out into the open many of the contentious issues which can brew up into real problems for the family company. Second, once in place, the agreement should provide a mechanism for side-stepping or resolving any disputes, or situations potentially giving rise to disputes, which come up.

The crucial problem which a shareholders' agreement addresses is that the legal framework which applies to all private companies in the UK often fails to reflect the actual relationship and aspirations of a particular company's shareholders – especially shareholders in family businesses or those which could be described as "quasi-partnerships". This chapter describes that framework, and then explains how it can be modified by a shareholders' agreement.

THE LEGAL FRAMEWORK

A shareholder in a private company will usually hold "ordinary shares" which literally represent a "share" of the company's net worth. Ordinary shares will normally carry voting rights, and will share in the assets of the company if it is wound up. Holders of these shares may also receive dividend payments, but will not have guaranteed rights to income. There may also be other classes of shares, such as "preference shares" giving preferential rights to dividend but limited voting rights, but in this chapter we are concerned with shareholders holding ordinary shares.

By law, control of the day-to-day activities of a company rests in the hands of its board of directors, who must act by a unanimous or majority vote. Shareholders holding more than 50 per cent of the votes attaching to the company's shares ("majority shareholders") can certainly pass a resolution to remove directors and appoint themselves or their nominees. But apart from this draconian remedy they have practically no rights to control the company's affairs, and shareholders controlling fewer than 50 per cent of the voting rights ("minority shareholders") have even less control over how the company is run (subject to a statutory "minority protection" remedy which is discussed below).

Shareholders who hold 75 per cent or more of the votes can not only control the composition of the board, they can also pass resolutions to change elements of the company's constitution such as its memorandum and articles of association. Theoretically (subject again to statutory protection) such shareholders could alter the rights of minority holders in a prejudicial manner (for example, by issuing further shares only to themselves and "diluting" the minority even further).

There are no legal restrictions on the transfer of shares in a private company. Unrestricted transfer can lead to one of the most common problems of the family company – shares passing, often on death, into the hands of people who have no direct connection with the business. As one generation succeeds another, shareholdings can become ever more dispersed, and this in turn can disrupt the running of the company. The disinterested shareholders may feel that they would rather have money than shares, particularly if dividends are not being paid. However, there is usually a very limited market for only some (as opposed to all) of the shares in a private company, especially if they comprise a minority stake.

There is a statutory remedy available to a shareholder who can show that a company's affairs are being conducted in a manner which is "unfairly prejudicial" to him or to other shareholders. This is a remedy particularly intended to assist in the case of the "family" or "quasi-partnership" company. The Court may make whatever order it sees fit; but usually where such cases actually come to Court the relationship between the shareholders has irretrievably broken down and the Court orders the majority to buy out the minority at a fair price.

THE SHAREHOLDERS' AGREEMENT

The purpose of a shareholders' agreement is to modify the legal framework described above in a way which is more appropriate for the operation of a family business, and also to anticipate some of the problems which can arise, particularly in relation to share transfers. It is essential that a shareholders' agreement should be carefully tailored to the circumstances of the particular company and each of the shareholders, but usually the document will deal with the following three principal areas:

- *"Management" issues – the agreement will contain provisions setting out the rights of shareholders, including minority shareholders, to be involved in the management of the company, perhaps merely by having enhanced rights to receive information, or more commonly by having rights of veto in respect of "restricted items", such as major changes affecting the company's business.*

- *"Constitutional" issues – there will be provisions which overrule the normal company law framework and require unanimity or a very substantial majority for changes to the articles of association, the issue of more shares, etc.*

■ *"Exit" issues – either as the culmination of a dispute resolution procedure (see below) or on their own. There are usually provisions which specify what is to happen if one or more shareholders wish to sell their shares, or if a third-party offer is received to acquire the whole of the company.*

Some of these issues are covered in more detail below, but the permutations are endless; the shareholders' agreement should contain only provisions which have been carefully considered and drafted to be appropriate for the company concerned.

TRANSFER OF SHARES

One or more of the shareholders may wish to sell their shares (assuming they can find a buyer). Common mechanisms in a shareholders' agreement will include:

■ *"Pre-emption" provisions - a shareholder wishing to sell must first offer his shares to the other existing shareholders, who may acquire them at a "fair price", and if several of them want to take up the offered shares, will do so in proportion to their existing shareholdings.*

■ *"Drag-along" provisions - if a significant majority (perhaps 80 or 90 per cent) of the company's shareholders wish to accept a bona fide third-party offer for their shares they can force any recalcitrant minority shareholder(s) to sell also, thus facilitating the sale of the entire company.*

Often the most vexed issue will be how a "fair price" is to be determined if it cannot be agreed between the shareholders. Commercially, shares representing a minority holding would usually attract a discounted price (assuming there was a buyer at all) because of their lack of voting control. However, it is common to specify that they will be valued proportionately to the valuation of the whole of the company's issued share capital. Even then, the valuation of a private company is as much an art as a science and the shareholders' agreement will usually delegate the task to a reputable firm of accountants.

DIVIDEND POLICY

This is another fertile area for dispute. There may be conflicting desires to retain money within the company for working capital and further investment, or to take it out for the benefit of the shareholders. The desire for dividend payments may differ between "management" shareholders, who can reward themselves with salaries and bonuses and disregard dividends, and "non-management" shareholders for whom dividends are the only way of receiving income from the company.

A shareholders' agreement will often set out the expectations of the shareholders in relation to dividends. For example, it may state that a dividend payment will be considered at least once or perhaps twice a year, and perhaps that profits available for dividend will be paid out after deducting an amount which the directors reasonably consider should be withheld as working capital. Alternatively a base level for working capital can be agreed, with any surplus profits over that level paid as dividend.

A typical shareholders' agreement will also provide that increases to directors' salaries and bonuses (or increases above a certain level, for example, which exceed the percentage increase of the Retail Prices Index for the same period of time), are a "restricted matter" requiring shareholder consent, to prevent "management" shareholders side-stepping the dividend provisions by simply over-paying themselves.

DISPUTE RESOLUTION

A dispute between the participants in a family business may well be much more bitter, and more difficult to resolve, than a similar dispute between the unrelated participants in a commercial joint venture. At worst, it may be impossible to manage the company effectively because constructive board meetings cannot be held. A company which is "deadlocked" in this way will certainly stagnate, and its directors may begin to run the risk of personal liability to creditors and others under insolvency law if their enforced inactivity leads to a deterioration in the value of its business and assets.

Simply going through the motions of a formal dispute resolution procedure, contained in a shareholders' agreement, can lower the emotional temperature and enable the substance of the dispute to be properly identified. Usually the parties will be required by the provisions of the agreement to identify the disputed issues in writing and submit them to a suitable expert – often a senior accountant or lawyer – for adjudication.

If a dispute really cannot be resolved, then the next step may be for the warring parties to indicate whether they wish to buy out the other shareholders and take control of the whole company.

If so, then there are mechanisms to resolve competing bids (including the exotically named "Texas shoot-out" and "Russian roulette" procedures). If not, then the very last resort may be a so-called "auto destruct" mechanism, which enables any shareholder to wind up the deadlocked company.

OTHER ISSUES

There is no limit to the topics which a shareholders' agreement may cover. Other items commonly dealt with include:

■ *Directors – shareholders or groups of shareholders may be granted the right to appoint "nominee" directors to represent their interest and give them some control at board level.*

■ *Employment – some of the shareholders may not be directors but may nonetheless expect employment. If so, then it is prudent for their expectations to be described.*

■ *Further funding – how will further funding be provided if required? In the case of a family company, the shareholders are unlikely to expect to be required to contribute monies and compulsory contribution provisions are unlikely. However, it may be helpful to set out the terms which will be granted to a shareholder who does subscribe further share capital, or who loans money to the company in response to a request from the directors.*

RELATIONSHIP WITH ARTICLES

Many of the provisions of a shareholders' agreement deal with matters which could be put in the company's articles of association. The articles are, of course, a public document. One reason for preparing a separate shareholders' agreement is to keep confidential the details of the agreement which the shareholders have entered into as to how the company should be run.

However, the relationship of the two documents must be considered very carefully and ideally they should be drafted together. In certain circumstances (broadly speaking, if the shareholders' agreement tries to deal with matters which should be the subject matter of the articles) all or part of the shareholders' agreement may be rendered ineffective unless it is filed on the company's public register at Companies House.

CONCLUSION

The constitution and management of a family company, which may represent the entire livelihood of some or all of its shareholders, is far too important to be left to the vagaries of UK law relating to private companies. A shareholders' agreement is practically an essential, not a luxury. It is astonishing how acrimonious, time-consuming, expensive - and often, avoidable - a typical family company shareholder dispute can be.

An "off the peg" shareholders' agreement, produced with little or no thought for the circumstances of the relevant company, may create as many problems as it solves. Shareholders should be prepared to use experienced advisers and spend enough time and money to produce a bespoke document which should anticipate almost all of the problems that the future may hold - not only for the current shareholders, but also for succeeding generations.

I must ask
Dad about
his plans for
retirement

For the well-being of everyone involved in the business it's vital to decide what will happen when the current management retire. ▌ Many will wish their children to take over the business, but are they capable of doing so? Will outsiders be needed? ▌ Grant Thornton can help you address these issues by drawing up a succession plan for the next generation of management. ▌ The insert opposite page **40** will tell you more about PRIMA – a new way of approaching these problems. Alternatively call us to discuss PRIMA on **0171 728 2720** or visit our website at www.grant-thornton.co.uk.

Grant Thornton ⬦

PRIMA

Chapter 5

Succession planning

Keith Tattersfield, PRIMA consultant at Grant Thornton, offers advice on devising a succession plan and securing the right successor

While planning for succession is likely to be unfamiliar and difficult territory to the business leader who is used to being the decision maker, it is a critical factor in ensuring that the business prospers into the future. As management guru Peter Drucker says: "The final test of greatness in a chief executive officer is how well he chooses a successor, and whether he can step aside and let his successor run the company."

The first question for the owner-manager to address is whether the business will be sustainable without him or her. Some enterprises are so dependent on the qualities of a single individual that succession isn't possible. If the business can be passed on, a range of issues need to tackled. For example, you may hope that your children will take over, but do they have both the aptitude and inclination to step into your shoes? Which child is best suited to lead the business after you've gone? Will "outsiders" need to be brought in to fill any gaps?

Succession planning should not happen overnight, it's a continuing process which should start long before you plan to retire. Plans should be seriously under way by the time the business leader is in his or her fifties and the children are probably in their mid- to late-twenties.

Putting the plan in writing will help to ensure that difficult issues are confronted head on, and that everyone in the business knows where they stand. The plan should include criteria for selecting the next generation of management, details of how successors will be prepared for their roles and contingency arrangements to cater for unforeseen events. The succession plan and successor should be widely anticipated by all involved in the business, and there should be no surprises.

CRITERIA FOR SELECTING A SUCCESSOR

The specifications of a succession plan must be clearly communicated to the family and management, with a detailed plan as to how and when the successor will be chosen, grooming and training requirements, and who will provide them. A timetable must be set for the transition and the succession process must be continually and closely monitored with sufficient flexibility to respond to changing circumstances. The following should be taken into account when developing a succession plan:

- *How to pass on the owner-manager's skills and contacts;*

- *The overall strategic plan of the business, encompassing the family's long-term objectives;*

- *Leadership and management responsibilities and the day-to-day decision-making process must be clearly defined;*

- *The qualities and skills needed for the future leadership of the business must be determined;*

- *The roles and responsibilities or "job descriptions" of potential successors must be clearly defined;*

- *The need to recruit a successor or an element of the succession team from outside must be considered;*

- *Career paths for all key executives should be mapped out;*

- *A specific programme should be set out, with definite milestones marking the path to succession;*

- *A contingency plan or "plan B" should be set in order to cater for any unforeseen events;*

- *Changes in the corporate culture and public perceptions should be addressed.*

When the successor is formally selected, it is vital that he or she is given the authority that goes with the responsibility of being a chief executive. This should be underpinned by an appropriate corporate structure, facilitating a smooth transfer of ownership and control.

FAMILY SUCCESSION

One of the most agonising experiences that any business faces is moving from one generation to the next. This issue is often most acute in companies where the founding entrepreneur hangs on as he watches others try to help manage or take over his business, while at the same time the heirs are feeling overshadowed and frustrated.

As family-controlled companies move into their second, third or fourth generation, they must recognise the dangers of indiscriminately promising employment to family members. Families should address these concerns by the development of specific employment policies for both family and non-family members, eg. individuals must have appropriate prior work experience and meet the requirements of the job. Entry criteria must be reviewed and discussed with the family members and with existing management – clear communication and fair application of the rules are more important than how strict or liberal the rules for entry are.

Fundamentally, family members should have a genuine commitment to, and interest in, joining the business rather than seeing it is a duty. As a general rule, family members should come into the business with between two and five years' experience of the outside world. This will enable them to gain self-confidence and a sense of independence. It will also bring a wider perspective to the business, thereby adding real value. It is also likely to enhance the individual's credibility in the eyes of non-family executives and employees.

Generally, entry should be into an existing and necessary job, with precedents for pay and performance expectations. All family members should have clearly defined areas of responsibility and should not directly manage other family members. If the single successor route is taken, steps must be taken by the parental generation to preserve family cohesion by helping disappointed candidates to recognise the reasons leading to the decision.

On entry to the business, the strengths and weaknesses of potential successors must be formally assessed and a training programme formalised, to enhance strengths and fill any gaps in the skills base. The chosen successor must be encouraged to think in terms of building a team, involving others in decision-making and welcoming input and feedback.

The timing of the successor's appointment as a director needs to be addressed, and should be seen as an important part of their development to be included in the succession plan. The company should incorporate appropriate "safety nets" to detect and counter the successor's mistakes by, for example, securing an active board of directors and a non-executive director.

On assumption of his new position, the successor is often faced with a "shadow" left behind by the patriarch, caused by the following:

- *Loyalty to, and dependence on, the founder throughout the organisation;*

- *A paternalistic loyalty which makes the implementation of change very difficult – successors feel guilty challenging the decisions of great predecessors, particularly if the predecessor was family;*

- *Success breeds organisational confidence in how things have been done and how the business is organised.*

The most difficult challenge for a successor is of respecting traditions while creating a culture of change. It is therefore important for successors to appreciate the above factors when addressing critical organisational issues, the aim being to preserve the values of the past, while assuring decision-making, innovation and flexibility for the future.

THE FAMILY SUCCESSOR'S DEVELOPMENT

The development of family successors should also be considered and planned for well in advance. To shape an individual's development, the grooming process needs to start when he or she is at an early and influential age. However, it is critical that you initially discuss whether the individual actually wishes to join the family firm and is likely to develop the required skills. The development typically follows seven stages:

1 *Preparation: a person's attitudes towards work are developed during their first 25 years. They may be shaped both through involvement in the business and externally.*

2 *Entry to the family business: usually occurs between the ages of 20 and 30 when the sibling, if entering the business, should be employed in an existing and necessary job which he or she is qualified to perform.*

3 *Business training: usually occurs between 25 and 35, when the successor should have a training plan and be developing the necessary skills and abilities.*

4 *Leadership development: usually occurs between 30 and 40, when the successor's plans stretch beyond their current job to leadership. The successor should develop team-building skills, while learning how to make effective decisions.*

5 *Selection: methods of making a choice include:*
   - *the emergence of a natural leader;*
   - *selection by the directors;*
   - *selection by the family;*
   - *consensus between the directors and non-family executives.*

6 *Passing of authority: the successor takes the helm and is responsible for strategic decisions.*

7 *Future succession: the successor should begin developing the next succession plan.*

CASE STUDY

In 1905 Charles Moore, managing director of Eastern Counties Laundries, gave a dinner party for his staff and family to celebrate the company's first 90 years in business. Without any prior warning he announced that he would be retiring – the next day. Everyone was taken by surprise, not least his sons who had to take over.

Despite Charles Moore's unusual approach to succession planning the business is still flourishing. His great, great grandson Dudley plans to retire next year, handing over the managing directorship jointly to his sons Tim and Anthony.

Each generation assumes the role of caretaker

Eastern Counties Laundries, founded in 1815 on the eve of Napeleon's escape from Elba, is based in Coggeshall, Essex. Today, it has five production plants operated by a staff of 350 and a turnover of £10.5m. Dudley Moore, the sixth generation of the family involved in the business, well understands the importance of planning for the future. "It never occurred to me to do anything but go into the family business" he says. "My sons felt the same way, but no member of the family should feel obliged to come in unless they really want to. The philosophy of our family is that each generation regards itself as a caretaker with the responsibility to improve the business and hand it on."

Dudley Moore started running the business in 1951 when he was 22. His father remained as chairman for some years, tactfully staying in the background even when Moore made "horrendous mistakes", such as trying to offset losses on the declining domestic laundering side by cutting out the ironing process. Despite these youthful experiments the company has flourished, with 99 per cent of its business now in linen retail.

Moore started planning the handover to his sons three years ago and made over shares to members of the family. Financial responsibility will remain in his hands while he is chairman, but production and the care of customers has been taken over by Tim and Anthony.

Don't hang on too long

"Put your succession plan down on paper, so you stick to it," he advises. "Keep everyone, including staff, informed of what is happening, and support and encourage the next generation. And above all, don't hang on too long."

Dudley Moore recently held a dinner to celebrate the company's second 90 years. His guests had no worries that he would emulate his ancestor's example. This Moore has the succession well-planned in advance.

ONE SUCCESSOR OR CO-SUCCESSORS?

Family businesses are often faced with the challenge of choosing a successor among several qualified siblings or cousins. The four structural approaches to this dilemma are:

■ *Giving one individual the final say;*

■ *Setting up separate kingdoms for each;*

■ *Having co-leaders; or*

■ *Bringing in an outsider.*

There is no single right answer to this issue. However, as a general rule, family businesses should choose one successor when there is one clear candidate. That said, fear of alienating family members often leads to one of the latter options being selected – different family members are put in charge of different parts of the business, with equal titles and equal pay. A common result is an unco-ordinated mess with the family arguing over functions and responsibilities leading to a power struggle, which is likely to result in the patriarch being recalled to perform a rescue.

For there to be successful co-succession, each successor candidate must be capable and prepared for leadership. This must be supported by shared fundamental goals and commitment, with each co-successor having areas of specific responsibility.

THE RELUCTANT PATRIARCH

Having built up the business, which probably equates to a large proportion of his life, the owner-manager may find it difficult to "let go" and retire. This can be exacerbated by being caught by the "trappings" of office – authority, respect and a salary.

The manner in which an owner-manager lets go is driven by his or her individual attitude. However, perhaps the most beneficial method to the firm – and diplomatic way for all concerned – is for the owner-manager to retire and act as a consultant to the board, while serving as a role model to the successor. In such a position, the retiring owner-manager can be used as a sounding board for strategic decisions, while maintaining low-level contact with customers, suppliers and employees concerned about management change. This should be underpinned by a clearly defined role for the retiring owner-manager, including the specific functions that he or she will perform.

OTHER OPTIONS

If succession is not an available option, other alternatives are to:

■ *Sell the business either via a trade sale or management buy-out;*

■ *Merge the business, either formally or by way of strategic alliance or partnership;*

■ *Float the business publicly;*

■ *Appoint an outsider to manage the business;*

■ *Wind up the business.*

The choice from among these alternatives depends on numerous considerations, including the perception of the external risks facing the business, the continuance of family involvement, the desire for financial liquidity and security, and the family creed.

CONCLUSION

Succession needs to be adequately planned, with appropriate training for the successor to enable him or her to take over the management of the company once the founder retires. One incentive for the owner-manager to address succession is that their presence within the firm is a powerful one and, hence, provides a basis for appointing an appropriate successor rather than bequeathing what is likely to become a significant problem to the next generation.

**Emotions can run out of control,
the business can't.**

PRIMA

Grant Thornton 🝍

P R I M A

PEOPLE AND RELATIONSHIP ISSUES IN MANAGEMENT

Owner-managed businesses are a thriving part of the UK economy. They benefit from the ambitions and skills of their principals and the close (often blood) relationships between members of the business. At the same time these very strengths can create weaknesses.

These weaknesses tend to be, unsurprisingly, where commercial and personal objectives differ. After all, a social group, such as a family, has different values from a commercial organisation. Inward looking, emotionally orientated and wary of change, the family is in many ways the polar opposite of the business.

As a result, the rewards that family members draw from the business, their part in managing it and their degree of control can all be areas of conflict.

The difficulty in resolving these conflicts may explain why fewer than a third of owner-managed businesses are passed on to the second generation and not even a tenth survive beyond that.

EFFECTIVE PROBLEM SOLVING

Grant Thornton is one of the few professional organisations to recognise the importance of relationships in business and to have developed

> I'm as sorry as anyone about William's accident – but we've still got a business to run. If it goes down no one benefits

a methodology for dealing with them, PRIMA.

PRIMA is an innovative way of solving problems in owner-managed businesses. It's effective because it looks at every kind of problem, not just financial ones and leads to an outcome which addresses individual, family and business needs.

A COMPREHENSIVE FRAMEWORK

The basis of PRIMA is a comprehensive framework which identifies key problem areas and the solutions to them. Significantly, PRIMA does not consider any of the factors in isolation but questions how they interact with each other.

A HUMAN APPROACH

More important even than methodology however, is the human aspect of our approach. After working with many owner-managed businesses over the years we know how sensitive the issues can be.

It's for this reason that your main contact with Grant Thornton will be an experienced partner in the firm.

Your PRIMA consultant will bring experience of other similar situations as well, of course, as objectivity and fairness. By working together we find the best possible resolution to any dispute, however insoluble it may appear.

Yes we need the new plant, but I'm not going cap in hand to the bank to get it

THE FRAMEWORK

ONE ▮▮ SUCCESSION PLANNING

When you're used to controlling a business the idea of passing that control to others may have little appeal. This is why many businesses are hampered by not having plans for the next generation of management.

Dad's business seemed to offer a good living. Problem was, my skills were so specialised I didn't have a lot to offer it.

Succession planning is a long term process which should happen long before the owner-manager plans to retire. Putting the plan in writing helps ensure that everyone – non-family executives as well as family members – know where they stand.

The plan should make clear how the next generation of management will be selected and prepared for their new role.

Contingency plans for unforeseen circumstances should also be considered.

TWO ▮▮ REMUNERATION PLANNING

When the emotionally based relationships of a family are put into a business context, the usual commercial relationship between contribution and reward can become distorted.

Salaries may be allocated equally amongst family members. Alternatively, pay may be influenced by the desire of the principal to see himself or his relatives prosper, rather than by market rate or performance in the job.

Practices of this kind can undermine morale and cause resentment – particularly amongst non-family employees. The solution will often be to separate the business from family loyalties and restore a common-sense relationship between contribution and reward.

THREE ∎ EQUITY OWNERSHIP BY FAMILY MEMBERS

Family members with shares in the business need to feel that they benefit from their equity. Yet they need not all be involved in the day-to-day management. The ownership structure should be clearly defined with an established policy for the transfer, valuation, acquisition and disposal of shares to ensure that equity rests in the right hands.

Simon gets twice my salary because he's the eldest. Sarah's had a pay rise because of the baby so guess who gets the least...

The question of dividends also needs to be considered. While a stable dividend pay-out is desirable, the shareholders' needs must be balanced with those of the business. To help manage shareholders' expectations, it is wise to have a dividend policy.

FOUR ∎ FAMILY MEMBERS NOT INVOLVED IN THE BUSINESS

The majority, possibly all, of your wealth could be tied up in the business. When it comes to an inheritance for your children, you may feel that the fairest course is to bequeath each an equal number of shares – regardless of their involvement.

Often such good intentions lead to conflict and disunity. To avoid this, it may be possible to find other ways of transferring wealth either out of the business or between family members. For example, a proportion of the business' value could be realised by selling part of it or you might wish to consider a stock market flotation.

Alternatively, you could create two classes of shares one with full and the other with restricted voting rights – the former being in the hands of those involved in day-to-day management.

If I put off making a will any longer, the tax man will be the chief beneficiary, but I'm just too busy to do it.

> I don't want people saying 'nothing succeeds like the boss' son'. If I go into the business I'll do it on merit.

FIVE ■ INTRODUCING AND REWARDING NON-FAMILY EXECUTIVES

A senior executive joining a family business will – not unnaturally – be anxious about the family's willingness to accept change and the contribution he or she will be allowed to make.

To recruit and retain high quality managerial talent, the family must be able to assure new executives that they will both play a key role and benefit from the contribution they make.

One way of achieving this is to create a rewards package which is directly linked to the performance of the business.

It was quite a revelation that meeting. It was the first time I realised that Gareth had no intention of coming into the business.

SIX ■ RETIREMENT AND ESTATE PLANNING

Planning for your retirement makes sense. If properly planned, a smooth transition to the next generation of management can be achieved. If not properly planned, retirement can be a cause of resentment both to those retiring and their successors.

The process needs to ensure your own financial security and also take account of changing circumstances.

SEVEN ■ BRINGING FAMILY MEMBERS INTO THE BUSINESS

As a general rule, family members should come into the business with between two to five years experience of the outside world. This will enable them to gain self-confidence and a sense of independence. It is also likely to enhance their credibility in the eyes of non-family executives and employees and allow them to bring a wider perspective to the family business.

It is important to define the responsibilities of each family member within the business. The basis of remuneration, criteria for promotion and training required should also be made clear.

EIGHT ▮▮ STRATEGIC PLANNING

Defining objectives is as important for owner-managed businesses as for any other kind. Many objectives will be the same: increasing profits and return on capital or long term growth for example.

What's different for the family business is balancing these goals against personal considerations. One of the purposes of strategic planning, therefore, is to define and reconcile these different objectives.

NINE ▮▮ FINANCIAL STRUCTURE

Financing is often a crucial issue for owner-managed businesses. In addition to meeting day-to-day liquidity requirements, you may need to fund capital investment projects and provide returns to family shareholders. The combination of these demands can place a heavy strain on the family business.

In theory I own 25% of the business, but I don't know if I could sell my shares or what would happen if I did...

Owners are often tempted to avoid external finance in order not to be indebted to outside investors or the bank. However, the effect of this can be to starve the business of the investment needed to maintain competitiveness or fuel growth.

To avoid these problems, financial structures should allow you maximum flexibility in running the business and be precisely tailored to your circumstances and needs.

The values of our business change according to whom you talk to. I think we need something more concrete.

The business can't move forward until we get everyone round a table and sort this problem out...

TEN ❚❚ PRESERVING WEALTH

If, as is likely, your business has accumulated wealth, how can you best preserve it?

A good principle is to create wealth which is independent of the company. By developing an asset base which is not reliant on the fortunes of the business, you will be spreading risk and paving the way for your successors to take the helm.

ELEVEN ❚❚ RESOLVING CONFLICTS

Lack of open debate is often behind serious conflicts in the family business. Potential problems over management control, succession and remuneration policy can turn into damaging disputes if they are not properly addressed.

It is never too late to resolve conflicts, provided the will exists to find a solution. What is needed is a commitment from all parties to follow an agreed procedure and abide by its outcome.

TWELVE ❚❚ THE FAMILY CREED

One way to help prevent or resolve conflict is to develop a family creed. A written distillation of the family's core values and principles, the creed might cover family members' obligations to each other, ownership responsibilities and attitude to risk.

Family relationships in business can, of course, be beneficial. Alternatively they may cause enormous difficulties. Grant Thornton have the methodology, the track record and the understanding to work with family members and deliver positive, profitable results.

FIND OUT FOR FREE HOW GRANT THORNTON WOULD VIEW YOUR PROBLEM.

Unlike more cut-and-dried business problems, relationship issues can't be reduced to a column of figures or a diagram.

This is why we have made a video to show how PRIMA works. It illustrates the kind of people and relationship problems which businesses face. You may find one or two of the situations uncannily familiar.

If you would like to sit down with us, face-to-face, we will be happy to arrange a free consultation where we can discuss how PRIMA can meet your business needs.

Simply complete the postcard below and post it (freepost) or call us on **0171 728 2720**.

It's time for me to take out what I need and leave the new generation in charge

Please tick here if you would like:
☐ **Free Consultation**   ☐ **Free Video**

If you would like more information on any of our core services, please tick the appropriate boxes:

☐ **Business advisory services**
☐ **UK and international tax planning**
☐ **Audit and accounting**
☐ **Corporate finance**
☐ **Corporate recovery**
☐ **Forensic and litigation support**

Name
Position
Company name
Company address

Postcode   Telephone
Fax   E-Mail

PRIMA

PRIMA

Anne Marie Tierney
Grant Thornton
(National Marketing)
FREEPOST NW5806
London
NW1 0YW

Chapter 6

Management roles

Hugh Jenkins, director of The Family Business Consultancy, assesses employment policies for both family members and non-family senior executives

The process of professionalising management decision-making and remuneration structures in family businesses can be a positive force for both the business and the family's health. When the principles are clear, understood and agreed on, and the psychological needs are matched with pragmatic implications, implementing effective change becomes more possible.

DEFINING THE PLAYING FIELD

Tension and the potential for conflict are inherent in any business, but particularly family businesses. Conflict will occur in family businesses between the individual's needs and the tasks essential for organisational survival. The greater the overlap of these needs, the more effective and efficient the business. How tension and conflict are acknowledged, mediated and resolved is fundamental to success and is a key issue in family businesses. The nature of the trade-off between family and personal interests on the one hand, and sound management practice on the other, is critical.

Family businesses present a particular kind of challenge where the owner and his identity easily become too closely identified with business. The family member working in the family business "has nowhere to hide", unlike the employee whose workplace is unrelated to home and intimate personal ties. The non-family senior manager faces different challenges, more along the lines of "having nowhere to belong".

One issue for all family business executives when dealing with senior staff is how to distance the family member from the family enough to be free to function efficiently, while at the

Do we really need a meeting about remuneration planning?

Yes!

The usual relationship of pay to market rate and performance can become distorted in a family business. ▮ A son may be over (or even under) paid simply because his father owns the business. Similarly, the father may continue to draw a salary after retirement. ▮ This sort of approach to pay can damage morale and the performance of the whole business. ▮ Through PRIMA we can help you put your remuneration policy on a commercial basis. The insert opposite page **40** tells you more. Alternatively call us to discuss PRIMA on **0171 728 2720** or visit our website at www.grant-thornton.co.uk.

PRIMA

Grant Thornton 🐦

same time including the non-family employee sufficiently for him to identify his professional future with that of the business. Decisions about management structures and remuneration are powerful ways in helping to achieve this balance. However, a structure that provides the freedom for family members and outsiders to operate effectively may also conflict with the belief system of the entrepreneur, who equates constraint with loss of autonomy and power.

COMMON MANAGEMENT PROBLEMS

Confusion about management functions frequently stems from problems in adapting to the changes in the business over time. What is critical to the success of a first-generation entrepreneurial business becomes problematic if the owner fails to differentiate roles and functions in order to professionalise it. The central role of the individual, his or her informal decision-making, and performance of multiple functions is incompatible with growth and the complexity that results.

This differentiation of function, and, therefore, the differentiation of "self" from the business, can be fraught with difficulty. It requires letting go, too often experienced as loss of control rather than as part of an essential developmental process. This shift requires identifying and separating levels of activity to match different people with complementary functions. In young companies the owner can hold the positions of owner, chief executive, manager, operations (and 'tea boy') all in one.

As John Tucker writes in *Entrepreneurs: Recognise any of this? (1995)*: The "very fact of complete psychological immersion of the entrepreneur...can lead to serious dysfunctional developments in the future in the case of continued growth of the enterprise". The functional levels that have to be unpicked are:

- *Directoral, that of developing policy and ensuring managerial tasks are completed;*

- *Managerial, strategic thinking and ensuring that strategy is carried through or modified in the light of experience; and*

- *Operational, the work at the sharp end. This is where clear thinking, planning and implementation of management discipline is essential, often in the face of irrational resistance: "We are different. We are a family business," is the cry.*

COMMON ROLE CONFUSIONS

Such thinking can lead to a confusion of ownership and management roles. Ownership, and therefore shareholding, is a family issue, while management and developing new products or services is a business issue. Management answers to the business and its owners, while the owner is responsible for the business.

INSIDERS AND OUTSIDERS

For the business to thrive long term, it must match the excellence that drives the business to policies which govern recruitment, evaluation and rewards for employment. Business owners often identify themselves closely with their "product" and are unable to see beyond this, as witnessed by favouring family members and a reluctance to consider outsiders to provide management skills.

Special qualities are necessary for family and non-family members to work successfully in this environment. It is important for a family member to establish himself in his own right with marketable skills, proven, if possible, outside the family business. The professional manager who works at a high level within the family business will need a particular psychological mindset because, whatever favourable options in terms of remuneration and shareholding are provided, he will never be a family member (by blood, even if associated by marriage), thereby remaining an "outsider". Even the most well-functioning family in business can fail to take account of this dynamic.

MANAGEMENT TENETS

"Be transparent!" This should be the watch phrase in all issues to do with decision-making about appointments, skills for the task and remuneration. Out of this flow all other principles. In family businesses it is the antidote to: putting off, avoiding conflict (sometimes by refusal to talk and sometimes by bullying behaviour), being arbitrary or secretive and blurring issues of difference, especially when difference is confused with "better" or "worse", family or non-family.

Rather than playing to strengths, hidden agendas distort decision-making and on occasion drive the business into the ground with all the accompanying personal and family pain. Business decisions based on primary family relationships rarely achieve more than short-term remission of problems.

CASE STUDY A

In the feedback from a communication exercise during a family workshop, a daughter-in-law said that for her there were a number of families. It was her husband first, then her family of origin, and then only thirdly this family into which she had married. Hers contrasted with other family members' views.

Challenging these assumptions allowed the unspoken to be acknowledged for the first time and also encouraged her to face up to potential sources of future misunderstanding that would adversely affect personal or business decisions.

If transparency is the starting point, the following can flow: clear analysis of business needs (as opposed to those of the family); identification of any skills gaps available from family members; and clearer decision-making about entry of family members into the business. No family member should join who is not free to work outside the business.

Terms of engagement should be the same for family as for non-family employees. Just as family businesses tend to take the longer-term view in the business cycle, so owners must take the longer-term view over employment. An appointment based on family membership can store up many or all of the following problems:

■ *Envy and dissatisfaction among non-family employees;*

■ *Loss of good non-family staff;*

- *Feuding within the family - both among those employed and those not working in the business;*

- *A replication of family conflicts in the workplace;*

- *Poorer business performance;*

- *Adverse effects on physical and psychological health.*

CASE STUDY B

A second-generation property company whose founder remained influential, but was no longer on the board, was looking to expand and needed additional staff.

At the same time, Jim, husband of eldest daughter Mary, was undergoing difficulties within his own business. Without a formal board review it was decided to take him into the firm as a senior manager.

Eighteen months later, Jim was not delivering. He was failing in the family business as he had previously in his own. A family-based decision to protect Mary's interests now compounded the problem for him and for the company. The three siblings were pitted against Mary and Jim, reactivating family feuds that had festered, having remained unresolved for years. Mary had 25 per cent equity and was a company director. She could not be bought out because the business did not have the cash, and Jim could not be fired because he was "family".

A chronic impasse had arisen due to lack of transparency in the appointments process and confusion over family and business priorities.

REWARDING NON-FAMILY EXECUTIVES

Professionalising the management culture requires the kind of forward planning which is counter to the early culture of young businesses of: "flying by the seat of their pants".

However, in the process of planning who and how to employ, the nature of the planning in the business will change. The effects are systemic. For the non-family director or senior manager there need to be clear reward structures, which may include equity ownership by those who have responsibility for governance and who play important strategic roles. This increases the likelihood of a longer-term perspective, while family control can be ensured by appropriate share buy-back schemes.

Equity, rather than annual profit-related performance bonuses, also encourages non-family senior managers to take a longer-term perspective and is likely to be more in keeping with the business philosophy and what the owners want to achieve.

However, if equity is not an option, non-family executives should be rewarded by pre-determined incentive schemes, ie. not through bonuses which are at the whim of the patriarch. Such incentives should either take the form of phantom share schemes or profit-related bonuses in order to motivate the non-executive to increase shareholder value in the long term.

The process of agreeing these decisions will help drive the business forward and increase the likelihood of attracting appropriate managerial skills into the business. Every post should be openly competed for. This sends critical messages to outside candidates and to family members who are considering joining, as well as to existing employees.

Prior to interview, clear criteria for essential and desirable skills must be agreed against which candidates will be judged, and the interview panel should always have the option not to appoint in the absence of a suitable candidate.

CAREER PROGRESSION

The establishment of an accountable management structure, equity ownership and other reward schemes are an important first step. There must be a formal appraisal process, applicable in equal measure to all employees – non-family and family – which is separate from promotion and remuneration procedures.

Without this, any family business owner should ask himself: "Would I really want to employ someone who is willing to come on board without such prospects?" When the answer is "yes", it may well indicate that the owner is not yet ready to have strong people in the team who will be willing to introduce independent thinking and professional practice.

At this point, the different systems – family, board and management – are likely to come together. It is worth noting that family businesses with active boards tend to have faster revenue growth, more disciplined business practices and more deliberate strategic planning processes. And what holds true at the top will filter down through the organisation.

Long before King Lear lost his eyes, he had lost his vision and his fitness to govern. The tragedy was threefold: personal, family and "employee".

The ultimate gift a parent can give a child is the skills to live independently and achieve satisfying relationships. Likewise, the ultimate test of leadership and of greatness is to bequeath a viable business independent of a single individual – founder or otherwise.

Chapter 7

Family members not involved in the business

Mark Watson, IoD corporate governance executive, identifies potential flash points caused by those family members who are not directly involved in the business

Family companies have unique qualities. Founded on family relationships, those involved in these companies tend to know why they are there and, perhaps not surprisingly, tend to win the loyalty of the families of employees. However, family companies also face unique problems, many of which can strain the family relationships and, in turn, adversely affect the company's ability to be competitive.

FAMILY STRAINS

The problems associated with family companies appear to stem from two sources. First, family members have a tendency to see their work and family life as one. With no distinct separation between the two, and no relief from the day-to-day work-related stresses, it can be difficult for family members involved in the company to stand back and assess situations objectively.

Second, problems are likely to occur as the company grows and is passed down the generations. Initially, the company's founder and close family may find that it is easy to chart the company's future, not least because company hierarchies tend to reflect family structures.

However, when considering the second and third generations, a wider family network becomes involved, and the once straightforward relationships inevitably become more complex.

In looking at the growth of the company then, it is important to address both the need to retain family commitment and cohesion, and to promote the company's success. The fact that only 30 per cent of family companies survive through to the third generation suggests that this balancing act can prove too difficult for many.

A GROWING COMPANY

As the company grows, the main potential problem area for family companies is the relationship between those family members who rely on the company for employment and those who rely on it for income, or both.

While growth can bring about major opportunities for the company, it can also heighten the tensions between these different family groupings. For example, those inside the company may feel that they are doing an effective job in running the company, benefiting those family members who do not contribute actively to its success. At the same time, those outside the company may feel that their views and feelings are overlooked in favour of those involved in the company's activities. Within this, perhaps the most difficult period of growth for a family company is the transition from being owner-managed to the stage where ownership becomes, to some extent, separated from management. For family members who are directors and those who are shareholders, the family dynamics change.

In essence, the growth of the family company means that the family relationships – once central to the company's success – have to transform into professional relationships. Family directors have to accustom themselves to their new roles, as do family shareholders. To complicate matters more, some family members will also see themselves as having responsibilities as owners in trust, holding and securing the shares for the generations to come.

Hence, the successful growth of the family company must be accompanied by a change in attitudes of the relevant family members, with all those involved being clear and explicit about their own and others' roles and responsibilities.

FAMILY REWARDS

One of the greatest challenges facing a family company are the difficulties associated with deciding how family members are to be rewarded for their contribution to the company – either as directors or as shareholders, or both. Of course, while the company is run by the original owners, the distinction between income from capital and payment for labour is somewhat academic.

However, as management becomes more distinct from ownership, it is essential to differentiate clearly between rewards from ownership and those from management, so that family relationships do not become too strained. While some family managers might think that in comparison with family shareholders they are under-rewarded, family shareholders may feel that family directors profit too much.

Even in situations where those closely involved in the company appreciate the differences between reward and employment, and income and ownership, their spouses and other close family members may not. As the wider family network becomes involved, particularly as the company is passed down through the generations, the perceived fairness of certain financial decisions may become an even more divisive issue.

FAMILY SHAREHOLDINGS

Another potential area of confusion and tension within the family relates to the value of each family member's shareholding, and the ability to realise its worth.

In many cases, family shareholders will only be able to pass their holdings on to each other. Even when their shareholdings are independently valued, this restriction on "sale" is likely to be taken into account in the valuation process. This raises the question of equity between family members. For example, those wishing to sell their shares may feel that they are undervalued and, therefore, feel that family members wishing to buy these shares are gaining unfair advantage. By contrast, in thinking of inheritance tax considerations, some family members may want to transfer the shares at as low a price as possible.

An independent valuation always helps. Those at the head of the company should seek advice on what options are open to them, such as a family trust. Such advice should highlight that there are more options available than either family-only sales or a full quotation of shares. The important element is making sure that family shareholders feel that they are able to realise the worth of the shareholding, and are aware of the means by which they can do so as equitably as possible.

OPEN, ONGOING COMMUNICATIONS

At the heart of managing family relationships within the business is the concept of fairness. Family divisions are as likely to be caused by perceived inequalities as by real acts of favouritism. There is a need to distinguish matters relating to the family from those relating to the company. In part, these problems stem from ineffective communications between those who are actively involved in the company's operations, and those who are not. Poor communications can, for example, cause problems at the point at which inheritance issues arise, as family members may feel cheated if they are unaware of why particular decisions have been made, especially those that at first sight appear inequitable.

If the family takes time to consider what future issues might need to be addressed, for example, a leading family member's retirement, it can plan a future in which everyone involved is clear about the aims, expectations and likely outcomes. The family must also be frank about how family directors are to be treated vis-à-vis family shareholders. The personal commitment of family directors to the company's long-term prosperity may mean that they are likely to be treated more favourably than family shareholders. The important factor is making sure that family shareholders are told why decisions are made.

Some of these communication problems, and the related perceived inequalities, can be addressed by appointing outside directors to the board. The issues surrounding the recruitment of non-family members to the board and at senior management levels is discussed in Chapter 6.

CONCLUSION

Family companies are likely to face some unique and complex challenges, some of which are highlighted above. However, it is clear that the need for open communications and long-term planning is of paramount importance to the success of family companies.

Openness will not, of course, resolve all of these potential conflicts. Interfacing the human and emotional elements of a family with the more objective, clinical needs of a company is likely to present unique difficulties. As always, it is a matter of judgement within the particular company and family situation as to the level of openness which is most suitable.

Yet, family companies could do more to forestall possible problems by insisting on a more frank and open dialogue between all family members concerned – especially between those who are involved on a day-to-day basis and those who are not. Planning for the future, including major changes in ownership and control, is vital. Finding out the expectations of all involved helps, as does defining ownership rights and responsibilities.

Above all, family members at the heart of the company must attempt to involve all family members concerned as much as possible, within the obvious commercial constraints. Leading family members, especially original owners of the company, must insist that such dialogue takes place and ensure that it is effective and ongoing.

Chapter 8

Strategic planning

Dr Allen Zimbler of the London Consulting Group, stresses the importance of strategic analysis in determining where the company is going, and keeping it on track

Family businesses are perhaps the most vexed by considerations of business strategy, particularly where business concerns are overshadowed by the family's requirements for the company, and when the identity of the business is merged with that of the family. In these situations, it becomes even more important to ensure that the business, as a corporate persona, enjoys the disciplined process of strategic planning.

In a world of complexity and change, there may never be obvious or easy solutions to business problems. The goal of a strategic process is to ensure that appropriate analysis and thinking takes place, and that considered choices are made between possible courses of action.

In this regard, "strategic" is best defined as making a significant change to a current course of action, or introducing something completely new. Anything else, in business terms, could be considered to be operational. The notion of "strategic planning", too, is something of a contradiction in terms. Given the rapid pace of change in the business environment, a plan could easily be out of date before the ink has dried.

Strategy should therefore be re-considered regularly and continually. The real challenge is to think. For this reason, participants in a strategic process should be those who are able to think beyond the historical and current mindsets prevalent within the business. They should also be able to engage in meaningful debate characterised by challenging and healthy controversy, without this being seen as a threat to the authority of the family that owns and manages the business.

If strategy is about learning what to do in the future, it is also about forgetting. What has worked in the past is no guarantee of what of what will work in the future, particularly as the business grows in size and develops through the stages of its own life-cycle. The best strategic methodology for the family business is one which is relatively uncomplicated, but which ensures that a systematic logic is employed which forces re-examination and commitment to decisions.

What follows is a model which will serve as a basis for a formal evaluation by senior management. Preferably, this should take place every six months, with monthly follow-up, in between. Ideally, sessions should be held off site over two-to-three days, to create a "mind space" away from the daily operational focus required by the business.

It is not always the case that the people who are best at the disciplined running of a business are also ideally suited to the requirements of a strategic process. If there is any doubt about this, an external facilitator should be brought in to assist. Whether in the management structure or not, family owners should be part of the thinking process about the future direction of the business.

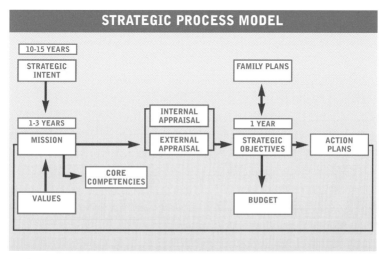

THE MISSION

The mission should be defined in a clear and succinct statement, that is easy to remember and describes the essential purpose of the business as well as locating its position two-to-three years hence. It should be compelling enough to be worthy of the best efforts of management and staff, and should also constitute a "pull" factor instead of a "push" factor in the business.

As the mission is a key element of a common meaning system, it should be arrived at by a process of debate involving senior management, ensuring that it is embraced by the management group rather than imposed on it. It also provides a criterion against which the appropriateness of decisions and activities can be tested.

STRATEGIC INTENT

Otherwise known as a vision, this should be a statement which envisions the organisation in ten to 15 years' time. This bold, but necessary, activity forces senior management to project the business forward into the future. While exercises like these obviously involve some degree of crystal-ball gazing, futures are not entirely unpredictable if features of the business environment are understood, and an analysis is made of what has been learned from the past.

Moreover, the accuracy of visioning exercises which base themselves on an imagined future is not relevant as long as the exercise is repeated frequently, so that changes in direction can be made to mirror changes in business opportunity. It is perhaps better to have a clear and common focus around a shared mission, even if it has to be changed at a latter stage, than to lack a common purpose. The challenge of leadership is to keep a business as vital as possible in order to minimise the possibilities of failure. Ongoing shared debate around the mission and strategic intent ensures this.

CORE COMPETENCIES

The core competencies of the business need to be identified and understood. These are the stores of knowledge, experience and practices which are unique to the business and which, collectively, form the basis of some competitive advantage into the mid-term. Technology alone would not be a core competence if it was easily replicable. A clear understanding of the core competencies of the business minimises the risk of pursuing business activities and directions which are not within the known capability of management. It thus maintains focus on core activities.

VALUES

Values define what is sacred and meaningful to all employees and, as such, provide a basis for the evaluation of the acceptablility or otherwise of decisions and actions, as they affect customers, suppliers, employees and stakeholders. Most business values are fairly universal and reflect widely-accepted codes of conduct and practice. It is, however, important to debate and define these, as values provide the backbone for a strong and wholesome organisational culture and, in the case of the family business, reflect the stated ethics of the founders.

A clear value-sense is strategic, in that it provides a means of harmonising the covert subterranean energies within an organisation, thereby minimising the effects of destructive conflicts and political agendas, negative attitudes and emotionally-based perceptions. This "informal" agenda of the organisation exists in every business, and, if not managed, can act to sabotage the formal agenda of a strategic initiative. Once values are set, they will obviously not have to be reformulated each year, as they should describe absolute standards, not relative ones.

INTERNAL APPRAISAL

A business thrives on its capacity to generate relevant information, and its ability to transform that information into knowledge.

Providing an ongoing measure of both the "hard" and "soft" aspects of organisational life and performance is crucial. The debate around what constitutes appropriate measures is as crucial as the process of ongoing measurement itself, forcing management to focus on what its levers of influence will be. Care should be taken to differentiate between criteria of effectiveness (doing the right things) and efficiency (doing things right).

Hard internal aspects relate to clear performance criteria, operating formulae, the appropriateness of systems and technology, the workability of structures, the adequacy of resources, and so on. Performance criteria should be kept as simple as possible, and as transparent as practicable. A system of ongoing measurement, with regular feedback and recognition of success, guarantees improvements in performance.

On the soft side, questions should be raised about the organisational climate, the level of morale, the incidence and nature of grievances, staff turnover, and the quality of management and supervisory management as perceived by people reporting to them. It is also essential to identify potential successors for key managerial and functional positions. It is quite possible to measure some of these dimensions objectively.

The internal appraisal thus addresses the internal health of the organisation, providing a necessary evaluation of its strengths and weaknesses.

EXTERNAL APPRAISAL

Opportunities and threats confronting the business must obviously be monitored continually. Within the context of the strategic process, these are discussed by the management team and examined in depth. It is sometimes useful to introduce external experts to the group at this stage in the process, as they challenge current belief and practice and provide information about changing industry standards and economic and business trends.

Two levels of analysis are useful. First, an ongoing macro-economic literacy should be maintained, monitoring the effects of socio-political and economic trends. An understanding of the behaviour of markets and confidence in the direction of the business cycle are essential to the management of risk in any business. Again, critical business indicators need to be defined and monitored, and "what-if" scenarios developed to manage contingencies. Second, an industry-level analysis is an obvious and essential source of strategic information. This should include both a competitor analysis and an ongoing comprehension of relative growths in year-on-year performance and market share, as well as benchmarking of one's own practices and performance criteria against industry standards and world's best practices.

In an era which can best be described as a technological revolution in the world, the information technology capability of the business is essential, whether it is in-house or outsourced.

A clear summary of both the internal and external factors confronting the business will enable an analysis to be concluded of the most critical strategic issues that confront the business. These need to be carefully defined, as they provide the basis for the setting of objectives.

SETTING STRATEGIC OBJECTIVES

In any one strategic management session, only four or five strategic objectives should be set. Practice indicates that this number is about as many new strategic initiatives as can be coped with at a time, without losing focus on the daily performance requirements of the business.

As suggested earlier, a strategic objective should answer a strategic need of the business – either by changing something the business has been doing up until this point, or introducing new direction or dimension in the business. While specifying measurable outcomes, strategic objectives should be broadly stated, and should be set with a time perspective of between one and three years.

At this stage of the process, it is essential to visit two critical points of reference. The first requires the evaluation of the stated objectives against family plans, to determine whether there is any obvious contradiction. If family members are part of the overall strategic process, this risk will be minimised.

Second, the strategic objectives must at this stage provide an input into the budget process. In many organisations the budgeting process is the only strategy employed. This is particularly the case with small and medium-sized family businesses, where strategic management skills may not yet exist in the business, and it feels somewhat threatening to hand over the process of determining strategic objectives to anyone else. As the process of budgeting is too often a linear projection of the company's history, it could even hinder real strategic possibilities. Where both processes do exist, they are often uncoupled, and run parallel and independent of each other. In such a situation, budget always constrains strategy. It is thus useful, from a timing point of view, to begin the budgeting cycle with strategic objectives as a substantial input.

DEFINING ACTION PLANS

At this stage each strategic objective needs to be made operational in the detailed action steps that will be required to achieve it. There are many examples of businesses that formulate "strategic plans", but fail to implement them.

In all cases, care must be given to assign each action step to an individual who will be held accountable for its implementation, even if other people are identified to assist. Rights of co-option must be guaranteed, and adequate resources allocated, including necessary time. A return date should be specified for each and every action plan, which should be tracked at monthly meetings against clear criteria for achievement.

CONCLUSION

The pursuit of strategy should not be characterised by mystique. Sound strategic management is by no means beyond the capability of the family business. The model outlined above provides a logical sequence of examination and questioning, thinking and analysis. By visiting the elements of the model on a bi-annual basis, management will force itself into a consideration of the strategic issues confronting the business and the determination of actions consequent thereto. The strategic process thus becomes another management discipline, whether an outside facilitator is used to guide the process or not. By being, essentially, an iterative process, it also becomes a learning process, adding enormous value to the growth and development of the business.

Chapter 9

Financial structures

Whatever type of family business you run, you will require an appropriate financial structure to nurture growth and development, says John Brown, assistant corporate director, Barclays Bank, Yorkshire and Humberside

Establishing a good relationship with your bank manager is especially critical for smaller businesses. Barclays' research shows that 86 per cent of them say their banks are their main sources of external funds.

As businesses grow, their financial needs become more sophisticated. The business needs protection against risk – whether it's from competitors, slow-paying debtors, a seasonal economic cycle, changes in interest or exchange rates, family disputes, illness or premature death. The key point is to arrange the most appropriate financial structure for your circumstances.

The company's financial structure should provide the maximum flexibility and fiscal efficiency, facilitate transfers of ownership and a positive cash-flow, and provide for taxation and inheritance tax. Failing to achieve these aims can cause major problems where a proprietor dies suddenly, especially as family businesses are often highly geared.

On questions of capital finance, your financial advisers should be able to counsel you on whether involving outside investors is wise, for example, given your long-term plans for the company, and if so, how much equity they should be allowed to take. They should also be able to help forecast the impact of the options outlined in this chapter on your gearing, credit rating and ability to grow the business, as well as their likely effects on the decisions of potential lenders.

Alongside these you should also consider other questions of finance, such as whether asset finance is more appropriate than taking out a traditional bank loan. Asset finance, through factoring and off-balance sheet vehicle finance, for example, can generate cash and make your assets work more tax efficiently.

FAMILY OWNERSHIP OR CONTROL

Research by Barclays shows that half the businesses with turnovers of between £1m and £100m are still owned and managed by their founders. But even where this is not the case, founders' families often continue to sit on boards.

So, control or powerful influence is often retained, despite complete ownership being surrendered. Issues of ownership and control are part of a wider question: how do you best provide for the future liquidity and capital needs of the business? The two overriding principles here are:

- *Be fair to all investors. Borrowing a large sum and buying out inactive shareholders, for example, may leave your company highly geared, which could be unfair to those who remain;*

- *If you fail to meet shareholder liquidity needs in a way likely to be sustainable, you could be encouraging investors to lower their sights and focus only on current returns. This will leave less capital for investment, which will weaken the business and reduce its cashflow.*

Any financial solution you choose must be adaptable to the needs of your business and should balance its liquidity needs with shareholders' desire for return on investment. When you implement your solution, you need to tell shareholders what it is and why you are using it. Internal and external techniques exist for meeting capital and liquidity needs. Internal techniques are the more common, as a family's wish to retain control of its business often makes it very reluctant to look outside.

MANAGING CAPITAL

The following methods of managing capital are available:

■ Controlling dividend rights

The proportion of earnings paid to shareholders periodically should depend on factors such as cash-flow, their expectations about returns and the yields available on alternative investments. Dividends can meet shareholder liquidity needs simply and predictably, but they drain capital from the business, and there is a tendency for recipients to see them as a right.

■ Staff share ownership plans

Setting up a trust that buys shares for staff, with company funds or borrowed money, can prove a great incentive to workers. But it could cost you a lot to set up, administer and audit; it will usually mean you having to buy shares back when staff leave or retire; and it could lower share values.

■ Divesting non-core operations

Distributing the business' assets among shareholders, usually by exchanging them for those in parallel firms or subsidiaries, can be beneficial although hard to structure. It may also damage family relationships where some shareholders own better performing assets than others. So it's essential to give all investors the same information and have the business valued independently.

■ Establishing a family bank

A family bank can be used to finance non-core business ventures, perhaps even supplemented by outside investors or sources. Family banks can help increase family capital through appropriate investment and encourage family members to work together. They do, though, redirect cash away from the core business and can sometimes spread the risks of new ventures to family members who may not necessarily approve of the investment.

RAISING CAPITAL EXTERNALLY

The following external solutions are available:

■ Bank loans

This debt, whether it be a bank overdraft, asset finance or a term loan, while being the most common source of finance is more often than not secured by a mortgage over the company's assets or, in some cases, by personal guarantees. Controlling the cost of borrowing means fixing repayment for a time when you expect the investment funded by the loan to be paying-off: family businesses sometimes unwisely use short-term credit to fund long-term investment. Although banks which lend can help businesses with cash-flow problems, through measures such as moratoriums on capital repayments and interest holidays, they will normally only do so where loans are long term.

■ Selling a non-core operation

Selling a non-core operation to raise cash for capital or liquidity needs may allow your family to keep control of its core business. It could, though, be hard to separate a non-core business for a sale which might, in any case, adversely affect your core business' trade.

■ Finding a private equity partner

You can sell shares to individuals or institutions, including venture capital funds and informal equity partners, such as those operated by some banks. This usually means the buyer is represented on your board and receives financial information about your business. Selling shares in this way provides liquidity without sacrificing family control; injects capital; and is cheaper and easier than a public offer or listing.

In addition, it may also introduce a minority partner, who may provide key expertise and services, such as advising on the long-term strategy of the business and supply a market for family members' shares.

However, a private equity partner is likely to expect higher returns than, say, debt finance and you may be obliged to buy out the partner in a specified timescale. It may also place restrictions on certain areas of the business.

■ A strategic alliance or joint venture
Adopting an alliance with a strategic partner can bring mutual benefits. It will allow you to become strong in more business areas than you could exploit alone and can provide capital relatively cheaply – through leveraging partnerships, different capabilities, greater market knowledge or enhanced management skills. But it also demands meticulous planning, including a realistic feasibility study, risk analysis, budgeting, due diligence and agreements to split rewards fairly; trust and adequate communication between the parties; partners avoiding a possessive attitude; and clear objectives.

■ Non-traditional sources
These include loans from the European Investment Bank, which are linked to job creation. They also encompass the UK Government's Small Firms Loan Guarantee Scheme, which is designed to encourage the growth of these companies.

DISTRIBUTION VERSUS REINVESTMENT

You need to consider whether the amount of money being withdrawn from your business to maintain family living standards is damaging the firm's long-term future. The following are ways in which to measure whether this is happening.

OWNERSHIP RETURNS AGAINST BUSINESS INVESTMENT

Family salaries and perks should normally not exceed 33 to 50 per cent of the company's net income before tax. That percentage should decline over time, even if more family members enter the business and earn pay rises, increasing the proportion of funds available for business investment.

FAMILY BUSINESS ANNUITY

This is the amount which the open market value of your company would earn if it were invested risk free. If the salaries, bonuses and perks going to your family total more than this, your business is being devalued and you need to take remedial action.

DEBT-TO-EQUITY RATIO

Repaying debts may sound sensible, but can mean denying your business necessary cash. Monitoring the debt-to-equity ratio will help you to avoid this mistake. Banks may ask you for covenants, which could include dividend and interest cover and committing yourself to a working capital ratio which prevents your business over-trading.

INSURANCE

You can cover obvious health risks through critical illness, key man and term assurance policies, for instance, to protect your business.

CONCLUSION

Never be too proud to seek expert help and advice on the issues mentioned in this chapter, because the consequences of mistakes can be extremely serious. Banks are the main sources of external funding to the vast majority of small businesses, so it makes sense to befriend yours. Even if they cannot meet one of your specific financial needs directly, the chances are they will have come across the issue before and will happily give you guidance or recommend someone they trust to provide a practical solution.

Chapter 10

Managing wealth and incentivising successors

David White, senior manager, growth and development services, Grant Thornton, advises on how to extract wealth from the business and, post-retirement, how to reward the executives managing the company

Once the business has matured and become sustainable, the family has often acquired wealth and should, therefore, ask itself a number of questions:

- *How should the fruits of the business' success be managed?*

- *Who will share in the wealth?*

- *How does one accumulate wealth outside of the family business without starving the company of working capital?*

- *Should wealth be available for contingencies or even security pledges on behalf of the business?*

In order to prepare for retirement, the family's wealth should be managed to provide financial security for the owner-manager, his spouse and dependants. Accordingly, the family should build wealth outside the company to develop an asset base which is not reliant on the fortunes of the business.

Further, if appropriately devised, the key family members will not be financially dependent on the business for their livelihood after retirement. This will enable successors to take the helm and provides an effective basis for estate planning. For example, wealth outside the business can be passed on to family members who are not actively involved in it, and shares in the business can be passed onto those who are.

However, when extracting wealth from the business it may be necessary to reconsider its financial structure, which historically is likely to have been funded by family capital.

BUILDING WEALTH OUTSIDE OF THE FAMILY BUSINESS

In order to calculate its net wealth, the family should list all of its assets and liabilities and then compare the value of assets tied in with the business with those outside it. Since the proportion of the family's wealth tied up in the business is often disproportionately high, a strategy should be adopted for the diversification and accumulation of wealth outside of the business.

Having listed the family's wealth, the business' assets and liabilities should be reviewed and non-core assets, ie. investments, personal assets and those for leisure and pleasure, should be identified. Non-core assets may then be extracted from the business in a tax-efficient manner, whether over a period of time or via a one-off transaction.

If it is not possible to extract wealth from the business, it may be necessary to sell a minority, make a public offering, or to sell out completely to secure the owner-manager's financial independence. In the case of the two former options, the family should consider the ultimate destiny of shares in conjunction with its long-term strategy and incorporate buy-back mechanisms where appropriate.

The management of assets outside of the core business should also be structured so that:

■ *An appropriate distribution to heirs is facilitated;*

■ *Inheritance tax is minimised;*

Similar to any financial investment, criteria must be established for investment requirements, incorporating the required asset mix and return, which should be underpinned by the individual's income requirements and risk tolerance levels.

ESTATE PLANNING

In both business and personal terms, it makes sense to plan in advance for retirement and for the transfer of your assets to the next generation. Doing so will enable you to minimise inheritance tax and make sure that there is a smooth transition to the next generation of management.

While you may be concerned that passing on wealth before you retire could jeopardise your own financial security, methods are available, such as pension schemes and trusts, to ensure that the path to succession isn't blocked by financial worries. Estate planning is a continuing process: current arrangements need to be reviewed whenever there is a major family event, such as a birth, death or remarriage; when there are changes in tax law, and every three to four years as a matter of course. The owner-manager should also consider key man insurance policies and, critically, his will; intestate succession is not recommended.

Owner-managers often have a joint will with their spouse which adopts the principle of "share and share alike". The "equal value principle" should be reconsidered in order to prevent the potentially problematic situation of share-owning family members who are not active in the business.

However, as hard as the owner manager may try to be fair to all the heirs, fairness differs in the eyes of the beholder, and conflict over inheritances is common, particularly when a business is involved. The principal cause of unhappiness is probably due to the assumption that fairness, by definition, means equal – when applied to a business it fails to recognise the differing interests of those children who are active in the business and those who are not.

Significant shareholders should know each other's estate plans and share transfer intentions, as they affect each other. In addition, sufficient funds must be set aside in order to pay the inheritance tax without impacting on the cashflow of the business. This will require determining the amount of inheritance tax payable, and then ensuring that there is sufficient liquidity to settle the potential liability.

REWARDING SUCCESSORS

Since the family is likely to retain a significant investment in the business, it should examine its management succession plans alongside the management of wealth, particularly when preparing for retirement. Accordingly, they should also address how to appoint the right calibre of executive and how to incentivise them so as to increase shareholder value, and hence the family's wealth.

To recruit and retain high-quality managers, the family must provide assurances that non-family executives in particular will play a key role in running the enterprise. However, perhaps the most effective way to alleviate the executive's fears and to provide a basis for a long-term relationship is to create a rewards package which is directly linked to the performance of the business.

Giving non-family members a direct equity stake, or other long-term incentives, such as phantom share options, will underline the family's commitment to these appointments.

It will also motivate the executives to work for the company's success over the long term. When discussing these issues the family should also formulate a strategy in case the non-family members leave or become incapacitated or sick, and consider the capital wealth being accumulated by them and how this is to be settled, either at the end of his or her tenure, or at an interim stage.

ISSUING SHARES TO NON-FAMILY EXECUTIVES

A family business should ideally provide equity ownership for non-family members who play strategic roles in the business. Equity ownership tends to give an employee a longer-term perspective, while cash bonuses tend to focus on annual profit performance.

In considering the question of whether to use shares as part of compensation, the advantages and disadvantages should be considered. The advantages are:

- *Family businesses have to compete for talent with public company compensation packages, which frequently include some form of equity participation;*

- *Issuing equity will reduce impact on cashflow;*

- *Alignment with the long-term goals of the business.*

The disadvantages are:

- *Relinquishing the "birthright" to shares;*

- *Impact on cashflow when the executive leaves or dies, and the company has to buy back equity due to there being a limited, or no, market for the shares;*

- *Concerns for the employee regarding the marketability of the shares;*

- *Opening of the family to scrutiny by non-family employees;*

- *The percentage ownership needs to be carefully considered in the light of the existing circumstances. A "safe percentage" of the shares must be determined, and ownership of these shares must be a condition of employment.*

The relationship between shares owned by family members and non-family executives should be clearly defined and a valuation formula and buy-back arrangement must be agreed in advance. This will minimise the possibility of a dispute and cushion the effects on cashflow if the executive leaves. If the family remains uncertain as to whether to issue shares, it may be necessary to issue a new non-voting class of share.

ALTERNATIVES TO ISSUING EQUITY

If the family is not willing to allow external equity, other mechanisms must be used to attract and retain talented non-family managers. But, whichever mechanism is applied, the objective should be to maximise the shareholders' wealth. Accordingly, the method of rewarding the non-executive should be predetermined with the capability of being measured against set performance measures.

Tools which are available include phantom share schemes or various forms of profit-related bonus arrangement. Alternatively,

Concept	Advantage	Disadvantage
Discretionary bonus	Encourages clear goal-setting and comprehensive review. Strengthens personal family ties	Rarely done well; usually uncomfortable for both parties. Others may be offended; can create paternalism
Annual profit bonus	Related to ability to pay and company performance	Not long-term orientated; profits can be affected by uncontrollable events
Long-range or multi-year profit bonus	Ties employees to the company for longer; encourages more long-term view	Profits aren't necessarily the most crucial measure (ie. return on equity, market share, etc.)
Phantom shares	Long-term orientation and related to shareholder benefit	Difficult to value for private company
Equity/share options	Long-term orientation and related to shareholder benefit. Confers greater emotional meaning or status	Complicated legal administration and difficult to value
Non-company investment opportunities	Strengthens personal/family ties. Doesn't affect company's share ownership	Not readily available. Any failure brings major disappointment

as a half-way house the company may issue share options to the executive. This will give both a performance-measured benefit to the individual and the advantage to the family of deferring the issue of equity until such time as tangible benefits are apparent.

The key advantages and disadvantages of the various forms of rewarding non-family executives are set out in the table above.

SUMMARY

To secure their own future it is essential for the family to have wealth outside of the business. To achieve this the business' financial structure must be appropriate and non-core assets should be extracted in a tax efficient manner. When the owner manager retires it is likely that a significant proportion of the family's wealth will be retained in the business and hence, they must adequately incentivise their successors to maximise shareholder wealth.